MEDITATIONS ON THE CROSS

MEDITATIONS ON THE CROSS

By
TOYOHIKO KAGAWA

Translated by
HELEN F. TOPPING *and* MARION R. DRAPER

WILLETT, CLARK & COMPANY
CHICAGO   NEW YORK
1935

232
K11M

26994
1951

TRANSLATOR'S FOREWORD

KAGAWA has published more than a hundred books in his own country. In other countries the demand for them is such that missionaries in Japan are banding themselves together to do the translation as rapidly as possible. Rev. P. G. Price, the outstanding leader in social work among them, has translated the last chapter of this book, on " The Cross and the Social Movement "; Miss Marion Draper, translator of a number of Kagawa's books and a member of his staff, the chapters from the seventh to the seventeenth; the writer the first six. Two theological seminaries offered their services to help in the process of final revision of the English text: Andover Newton at Newton Center, Mass., and the one at which the work is being completed. Especial thanks are due the hospitable generosity of Dr. C. C. Cunningham, acting president of the latter, and to Dr. A. C. Tandy, a student of Dr. Shailer Mathews, and its professor of homiletics. With deep spiritual insight and balanced theological judgment, the latter has scrutinized the text in an effort to fit it to American thinking, meanwhile preserving a fine loyalty to the author. Mrs. Dameron, Mr. Rose, and a number of other students of the Kansas City Baptist Theological Seminary have contributed the secretarial help.

These pages present a sort of threefold Kagawa: (1) as evangelist preaching to Japanese, the majority not Christians, so that there are Japanese words, illustrations, Biblical references, and a certain amount of repetition of material and thought; (2) as social prophet, insisting on the service of religion to the cause of social solidarity;

(3) as great Christian, meditating for himself on the greatest fact in human history. The first six chapters might be called " The Cross in the Scriptures "; the last twelve, " The Philosophy of the Cross." The American reader who yields himself to the difficult task of intellectually and mystically laying hold on Kagawa's concepts in the first part will find his faith rewarded; both as he reads the later pages in the relative ease with which he understands them, and in finding his mind implemented for social reconstruction after closing the book.

It has been suggested that chapters five and six on Paul might be read before chapter four, which may be to some the most difficult, dealing as it does with the Fourth Gospel. After seeing through Kagawa's eyes the bourgeois nationalist intellectual that Saul was, converted into the best interpreter of the proletarian Jesus, one is prepared to find other bourgeois following him in repentance and conversion, as they do in the Fourth Gospel. To Kagawa this much debated document is largely a compilation of the confessions of officials who crucified Jesus and afterward repented of it.

This makes it of importance as class literature for oppressed proletarians. Kagawa does not care who coordinated the fragmentary recollections of Nicodemus, of Joseph of Arimathea and of the others who made their confessions as they joined the Christian community, or at the annual memorial services on the anniversaries of the crucifixion. But having himself suffered repeatedly the agonies of unjust arrest, trial and condemnation, he recognizes the typical character and also the psychological soundness of the scripture records; and he knows that nothing, to persecuted proletarians, can take the place of the consolations afforded by these confessions of their converted oppressors. It is Jesus as not merely a typical proletarian, but as a proletarian of the proletarians, the most oppressed of all, who is presented in the Fourth Gospel. In the period of reconstruction and consequent persecution that is upon us, we shall re-discover the Fourth Gospel, Kagawa says, as a spiritual foundation for present-day prophetism.

Formerly religion was called opium in Russia and with some reason. Kagawa is freeing Christianity from the enslavement it has suffered to bourgeois materialism, partly by re-interpreting its own records, obscured under the minutiæ of bourgeois theologians of the last two centuries, who spent their lives in their capitalist-supported libraries and therefore did not understand their Bibles. Kagawa says that in order to do so it is necessary to get down into the social movements of the poor in which the Bible grew, the movements for human emancipation. The reader who grasps his thought will be the one who sees in the following pages the emergence of the gospel for the working classes, for the cooperative movement, and for all those who give themselves to sacrificial service for economic and social reconstruction. To such the Cross is not a theological dogma but the only possible Way of Life.

HELEN F. TOPPING

KANSAS CITY BAPTIST THEOLOGICAL SEMINARY
    October 11, 1935

CONTENTS

MEDITATIONS ON THE CROSS

INTRODUCTION

I

O Son of Man, bearing the cross upon his exhausted and
bruised shoulders, climbing the hill of Calvary, I myself
have seen him!
　　Weighted down by the burden, in the road he falls.
　　Then Simon the father of Rufus,
　　Hurrying up to the spectacle to gaze upon it
　　Is pressed into service by the soldiers.
　　He, the astonished countryman, grumbles not a little
　　As he shoulders and carries forward the unwelcome
　　　　burden.
　　Thus desires our Lord Jesus of us, that we, too,
　　Take our turn in bearing his cross.
　　For Jesus, after three years of unresting struggle,
　　After uncounted nights of prayer, and in particular,
　　After the last night of agony in Passion week,
　　Jesus, the sturdy manual laborer that he is,
　　Has no more strength in him
　　To carry the cross alone.

II

Steadily he guides himself along the road of his destiny
That, having saved others, he may not save himself.
For, in the name of religion, the ruling classes
Are carrying on a system of exploitation.　Thus for one
Who lives in the love of the Heavenly Father
There can be no avoidance of the direct conflict with
　　them.
He who would save the lost sheep may not shrink

3

From being himself devoured by the wolf. Determined
To walk the great highway of holy suffering,
In order to live in the love of the Infinite,
He willingly abandons himself to the cross.

III

As in the flowering of a maiden there are stages
Between babyhood and the Day of the Bride,
So in the growth of the race there are historical epochs.
The seed sown in the earth sends forth a sprout,
Then a bud, then a blossom, and at last the fruit.
Thus in the history of mankind there came a time of
  great fruition.
Driven from the Garden of Eden, the sons of men, still
  dreaming,
Stumbled half awake at early dawn;
Then after a long interval came to full consciousness
Of redeeming love and the grace of God,
And through Christ bore their first fruits.
He it is who is indeed the Son of God.

IV

O winter weather of the human race! After your cold-
  ness
Came the springtide of Love Omnipotent!
The Omnipotent Love of the Universe —
It is its fruitage that we see in Jesus.
Christ is the first man to awake to full consciousness of
  the Universe,
The first to realize his responsibility even for sinners.
But as winter comes back again after the fruit-bearing
  of the flowers
So, since the Flower of Love blossomed in the bosom of
  Jesus,

Humanity's winter has come round again and again in
    wearying repetition,
Nor since then has there yet appeared on earth
The flower of Universal Love like that of Jesus
Brought to blossom and fruition in a group, in a com-
    munity.

V

My heart is grieved within me at human degeneracy
And at the weak, poor-spirited life of the human race!
Compared with the lofty figure of Jesus
I am disgusted with my poor self!
In this mood Paul longed to have his old self
Crucified on the cross with Jesus.
Before asking it of others, I, too, would crucify myself,
And living henceforward not for my own self,
Would awaken to the Love of the Universe,
As it continually dies for others.

VI

The sphere of Nature is a world of never-ending love.
Without love and sacrifice it would be impossible
To sustain this marvelous Temple of Life.
This law of love is unchanging even in
The realms of mammals, of birds, even of insects.
But these worlds the scientists point to
Are those of mere instinctive loving; through Christ
We discover that which goes beyond instinct —
Redemptive love for the first time attaining its freedom
And awakening as a human being!

VII

This Redemptive-Love-World is the only region
In which a holy society can be created; and yet

Autocrats and social revolutionaries, capitalists and
    communists,
All treat as nonsense this Cross-consciousness
Which rises beyond instinct. Without it,
Without awakening to this full Cross-consciousness,
The social revolution is absolutely futile. He who hesi-
    tates to enter
His chrysalis will never become a butterfly.
Social creation is utterly impossible except by
Traversing the Via Dolorosa of the Cross.
In the history of the human race there is needed
The creation of this Cross-consciousness,
That is to say, the creation of
The inner life of its very soul.

VIII

This is not a Way of petty superficial devices — it is a
    Way
Marked by blood, and the pouring out of
Life's volcanic eruption!
It is Life's highest art, this most courageous loving,
Reaching up to Heaven through the life-instincts;
It is the adventure of ultimate Love;
It is the consummate Art of the Universe.
Without it, the history of the Universe is equal to simply
    zero.

IX

As in a single Word, Christ's Love-Movement
Is summed up in the Cross. The Cross is
The whole of Christ, the whole of Love.
God speaks to man through the Cross
Of Love's mysteries concealed in the Divine Bosom.

X

Leave to the Greeks their theories of Divinity!
Abandon to their musty libraries those scholars
Who fail to love humanity, and prefer ivory pagodas!
Those who have no love of humanity
Have no way of knowing the Love of God;
The knowledge of the Love of God comes only
By way of the Bloody Cross; he who fears to bear it
Cannot know the Love of Christ. Bathing in the blood
Flowing from the side of Christ
We must continue today's struggle for love.

XI

Is your love-citadel completed, friends?
Have you entered into your rightful inheritance
Of death to self and service for others?
Have you done your portion of road-breaking
For the Way of the Cross — among the lepers,
Among the tuberculous, among the barbarians of
    Formosa,
Or along the icebound straits of the Northern Seas?

XII

Without the Cross there is no victory.
Give way neither to weeping nor to cowardly violence;
Before pointing a pistol at others, subdue your own
    spirit!
Press forward, O Cross! Make world history over
Into the history of the Cross! Without the Cross
The real uplifting of humanity is impossible,
No matter how the upper structure of society may vary.
Press forward, O Cross, press forward!
Fearing neither the abuse of men nor their threatenings,

Let us go forward!   In the blood-drops dripping
Along the sorrowful road of the Via Dolorosa
Will be written the history of man's regeneration.
Tracing those blood-stained and staggering footprints
Let me go forward!
This day also must my blood flow, following
In that blood-stained pathway.

TOYOHARA INN, KARAFUTO.   (Southern Saghalien.)
     May 25, 1931.

THE SECRET OF THE CROSS

Then he warned the disciples not to tell anyone that he was the Christ. Matthew 16:20.

TODAY it is very easy to talk about the Christian religion. And we take it for granted that Jesus went about talking about his being the Christ. Jesus, however, never once said that he was the Christ! Even when the disciples said to him, " You are the Christ," he said to them, " Don't tell it! Keep it a secret! " This is what I call the secret of Christ.

Why did Jesus not let people say that he was the Christ? It was because he was not yet qualified to call himself the Messiah. Until he took the Cross he could not be the Christ, he thought. To us this fact is unexpected, strange, startling. Unless we study the Bible well we fail to understand this.

When the Salvation Army leader, General Booth, came to Tokyo, a certain man went to the station to meet him wearing a banner on which were inscribed the words, " Buddha — Christ." He maintained that he himself was the Christ. But no one believed him. About that time I met that man frequently, and knew him to be a quiet and fairly docile person, although so deeply self-deluded. He thought it was his duty to advertise himself as the Christ.

Quite recently another Japanese announced that since there were six moles on the back of Christ, and six moles

also on his own back, therefore he himself must be the
Christ!

There was nothing of this sort of self-display in Jesus.
Jesus was extremely modest. When John the Baptist sent
him a letter from prison by messengers asking, " Are you
the coming Messiah? " Jesus could not answer, " Yes."
If he had been like that Japanese he would certainly have
answered, " Yes — the proof is that I have six moles on
my back! " But Jesus said, merely, " Go and report to
John what you hear and see. The blind are regaining their
sight and the lame can walk, the lepers are being cured and
the deaf can hear, the dead are being raised and good news
is being preached to the poor. And blessed is the man who
finds nothing that repels him in me."

Jesus could not say more than this. He did not go
around announcing that he was the Christ. In his in-
herent nature lay his power to help the distressed. At this
point lies the difference between the Christianity which
does, and that which does not, advertise itself.

THE CHRIST WHO DODGED THE REVOLUTION

Up to the age of thirty, Jesus kept silence, and worked
at the carpenter's trade. Then he cast aside his saw and
chisel and became a disciple of John the Baptist. After
that for about a year he traveled around with John. In
the spring of his thirty-first year, when John was cast into
prison, the course of Christ's life changed. From that
time onward, for just about a year, he pursued his remarkable Galilean ministry.

At first he was working alone, but later he sent out
twelve disciples and did an extensive and vigorous piece
of evangelism.

On the night of King Herod's birthday, John the Baptist was beheaded. At that a revolt broke out. The mass

of the people wanted to make Jesus king. (John 6:15.) This is written in John alone; not in Matthew or Mark. Therefore John's Gospel is of great importance in telling the life-story of Christ.

We moderns think of the feeding of the five thousand, and later of the four thousand, as mere miracles performed by Christ, but we ought to realize that behind those miracles lay the above-mentioned situation. When John was killed the people became infuriated and cried: " Down with the tyrant Herod who killed the prophet! " And the revolutionary party thought that if they lost that chance they would never have another such favorable opportunity in which to strike.

Most people see only the religious side of the scriptures, and do not grasp their underlying social factors. Being involved in the social movement as I am, I cannot but see the social side of the Bible.

To become the leader of five thousand revolutionists seemed to Jesus a very foolish thing to do. So he set out on a journey from Capernaum to Tyre and Sidon and back again. Upon returning, several months later, he investigated the situation very quietly, thinking that by that time the revolutionary ferment must have died down. He found, however, that the revolutionists were still active. At that time King Areta of Moab was coming to invade Judea with fifty thousand in his army, because his daughter had been divorced by Herod Antipas. Probably because of that circumstance the number of revolutionists was smaller than before, but there were still four thousand who came together at Jesus' return.

When we read the Bible in the customary way and discover these statements that Jesus first fed the five thousand, and later the four thousand, miraculously, we dismiss them as merely " two more miracles." We need to know that behind these statements is the situation described above. As to why the scriptural accounts are not more explicit, it should be sufficient to explain that at that time it would be dangerous for any author to refer to the abolition of the kingship or to the rights of the common people. He might fully expect to lose his head as well as to have his book suppressed by the government.

Yet the people came together for three days with Christ, intending to hold a secret parley with him about a revolution. If Jesus had acceded to their wishes they certainly would have followed him. Instead he said, " Think of Moses! If you think of Moses, does not that make you realize that a revolution would be very foolish? " He rejected the advances of the five thousand and went on his journey, and later, on the second occasion, rejected the pleas of the four thousand and again went on his way.

TALKING OF THE CROSS

During this journey, thinking that the people must be calling him a coward, Jesus asked the disciples what the crowd was saying about him. They replied, " Some say John the Baptist, others Elijah, and still others, Jeremiah, or one of the prophets." He said to them, " But who do you say that I am? " In other words, he asked, " Then what do you fellows think? " and Peter answered promptly, " You are the Christ! "

At that Jesus said, " What an extraordinary thing you are saying, Peter! God made you say that. But you fellows must all keep it a secret." And at once he told them that he was to be put on the Cross. But the disciples thought that he was to be King, and to reign over the world. And here was Jesus himself saying that he was to be put on a cross!

Possessed with this idea that Jesus was to rule the world,

and to promote the members of the twelve to high positions like glittering stars in his firmament, Peter protested to Jesus: "Rabbi! Don't say such a depressing thing — that you are soon to be executed!" And Jesus scolded Peter: "Now you are thinking differently, like a man, not like God! Get away from me! Satan!"

To the very end the disciples failed to understand this.

There are two kinds of Christianity: success-Christianity and failure-Christianity. Jesus said, "Unless I fail, my work will be useless." It is, however, a fact that when anyone becomes a Christian there is the danger that he may become too successful! He does not drink nor smoke, he possesses the confidence of his fellows, so there is nothing left for him to do but to succeed. In contrast to that, Christ said a very gloomy thing; he said that he was intending to fail!

Meanwhile the disciples were thinking merely of how they themselves were to be elevated to high positions as members of his cabinet. On their way back to Capernaum from the second journey to the north the disciples were thinking of nothing but such things and were ashamed to confess them, so Jesus taught them, "You fellows must become babies!" And when he was on the way to the evangelization of Perea, the mother of James and John brought her two sons and appealed to him to put her children one on his right and one on his left as chief cabinet ministers, when he should become the king. The other disciples were extremely angry when they heard of this, because, (as they probably said) "James and John even took their mother to Christ to make this request for them!" Up to the very eve of the crucifixion the disciples were indulging in quarrels for place and position. Luke 22:24 pictures this last scene.

Thus while moving about from place to place, from the

time Jesus returned from his northern trip to his last hour on the Cross, the disciples failed to comprehend his secret. Why did they fail so? Because they thought he was to become an earthly king! They did not grasp the profound thing that he himself was contemplating, that he was to be put on the Cross according to the scriptures, as a sacrifice for all men. His teachings and his deeds they understood, but they had no comprehension whatever of his inner consciousness.

Modern theologians are mostly like that.

THE CRISES OF CHRIST

From the social point of view there were two crises in the life of Jesus. One was at the time of John's imprisonment and the other when John was executed. Though himself possessing a superior conception, Jesus took it very seriously when John said of him, " Behold the Lamb of God which taketh away the sin of the world." From that time forward Jesus assumed the attitude of kingship, that is, of a king who was to bear, as a sacrificial lamb, the sins of his people. Therefore from that time on Christ's oppression by the governmental authorities increased. There were three causes for his arrest: first, *outward condition,* or the objective situation; second, *governmental oppression;* and, third, *Christ's own consciousness.*

Why did Jesus have to be crucified? According to the explanation of the court, it was on three charges: Treason; Blasphemy; Disturbing the peace (violation of the Peace Preservation Law).

Jesus could not escape from any of these accusations. To the governmental authorities he was indeed a dangerous person. But he did not himself intend to become a king. When Pilate asked, " Are you a king? " Jesus did indeed answer a simple " Yes," but the meaning in which he used the word " king " was entirely different from that of the politically ambitious disciples.

Why was it that when asked this question by Pilate, he answered in the affirmative? Well, the situation was something like this. Pilate had inquired, with a sort of impartial detachment, " Is it true, as the chief priests say, that you are the king of the Jews? " Jesus answered, becoming bolder as he faced the court, " My kingdom is not a kingdom of this world. Governor, please don't misunderstand me! If I were talking of an earthly kingdom, my own countrymen would not approve." At that Pilate replied: " For the life of me I can't understand you. Are you a king or are you not a king? "

So, when he reiterated his question, Jesus answered, " Yes."

This is a short but very significant passage. The kingship Jesus was talking about was the kingship of the kingdom of truth, and he was saying that he was the king of that kingdom.

" Then what is this ' truth ' you are talking about? "

Pilate has grasped that this kingship Jesus was referring to was an abstraction; that he was a king in an abstract sense. So he reported, " This Jew is a thought-criminal, but there is nothing to touch his thought-crime in Roman law."

Therein lies the great reason why Jesus had to be tried.

CONSCIOUSNESS OF REDEMPTION

But what was the inner consciousness of Christ? Without an understanding of the meaning of the lamb in Jewish ceremonial one does not grasp the consciousness of Jesus. Ceremonials were many in Palestine, and one of the most characteristic of them was the Purification Festival on July tenth, when they made cleansing for the sins of the entire preceding year. Moreover, such purification from sin is not understood except by persons who understand what sin itself is.

If he had really wanted to be a king, Christ could have been one. Since as many as five thousand followed him, had he once lifted his banner, he might have led a successful revolt. But instead of the wish to lead a revolution, there was in the consciousness of Christ the will to make up for the deficiences of others to save them — the solidarity-responsibility consciousness.*

We can in a measure understand this from our own feelings today. Though I myself do not have the memory of having told a lie, or of having done anything wrong, and though I think myself innocent, yet when anyone else commits robbery — especially where such a responsible personage as a cabinet minister commits a crime and is thrown into prison — I feel a relationship to that crime, and that I must ask forgiveness of God for it. The Jesus who thought like that was truly the King of Truth.

The kingship of Truth becomes God-consciousness. One bears the faults of others on his own shoulders and asks forgiveness of God for them, as if they were his own. Jesus thought that unless he did that he would not qualify as a king.

Jesus was not merely an ordinary king. He was a king who, being a man, had God-consciousness, and be-

---

* "*Solidarity-responsibility consciousness.*" The Japanese are strongly imbued with this feeling of social solidarity. It appears in a negative form in the Old Testament. The Hebrews thought of the family, the nation, rather than of the individual. Achan's sin caused the defeat of the whole army, and the death of his entire family. In the New Testament, Paul's " body " chapters, 1 Cor. 12, Rom. 12, and Eph. 4, illustrate the growing conception of positive social solidarity in the Christian community.

ing God, had human consciousness. A king cannot resign. A king has absolute responsibility. In this sense, Christ is King of the human race. He must undertake the responsibility for this task. Students and learned men who have never undertaken to bear the consequences of the failures of others find it impossible to grasp this. Such academic recluses, while continually talking in a censorious way about the faults of others, have not the slightest intention of undertaking to bear the consequences of those faults on their own shoulders.

This, then, was the secret of Jesus Christ. And this we can fit into our daily lives. And advancing one more step, taking the "filling up of the measure of what is lacking in the suffering of Christ" as our responsibility, we must make the world's sorrows our own. That is Christianity. The moment we ourselves are saved, we must set ourselves to saving others. The way Christ became the Atoning Lamb was by his hanging on the Cross and dying there. And Christianity for me means to dedicate myself to serve others even unto death. That, I am convinced, is the true Way of Jesus Christ. Christianity means to save others. That is the way of the Cross, and the true way of Christ.

PRAYER

Father God: We thank Thee that we have been enabled to meditate on the Secret of Christ. As He chose the death of the Cross, fully embracing its ultimate bitterness, we too will walk the narrow path, chained to the Cross. Since this unworthy servant of Thine will henceforward move only as bound to the Cross, I beseech Thee to lead even me in the Way of Christ. Through Christ we pray. Amen.

II

THE CROSS IN THE CONSCIOUSNESS OF JESUS

*The Son of Man came not to be ministered unto but
to minister, and to give his life as a ransom for many.*
Matthew 20:28.

THERE is a famous cathedral in the city of Gloucester,
England, built eight hundred and fifty years ago and very
beautiful. In its crypt lies the body of King Edward II
arrayed in full armor. Up to a hundred years ago it was
the custom for pilgrims to pass through the little door into
the crypt and walk around the body of King Edward, and
even today his name is not forgotten.

Edward II was the hero of the first great Crusade, and
the Crusades are historic. There are many crosses on the
walls of Jerusalem carved by the Crusaders, who attempted to regain the land of the Savior — snatched away
by the Mohammedans. Through more than a dozen of
these Crusades, over a period of more than two hundred
years, and despite repeated failures, they continued in
the effort, and many gave their lives in the attempt. They
carved their crosses as a sign of their sacrifice and self-
dedication.

The Crusades were of course an extremely crude expression of Christian devotion. And yet, out of the very
midst of this warlike period, with armies on the march all
over Europe, grew one of the significant phases of the
Christian Brotherhood Movement. Many of the Cru-

saders helped the poor and practised the brotherly kindness of the Christian church. In Florence, for instance,
Crusaders at this period went out to look after the sick
who lay ill in the streets. They put masks over their
faces so that others would not find out who they were.
We need today the spirit of the Crusader-nurses who put
masks over their faces in old Florence.

I am against war. But I feel the glamour of the brave
samurai spirit of the many hundreds of thousands of
men who fought, not to regain territory or to hunt treasure,
but for one single purpose, to win back the tomb in which
Jesus was buried. While the crowds today seek night
life and gambling parties I admire the sacrificial spirit
of those who gave up honor, wealth and security to undertake a more than hundred day journey from England
to Asia Minor.

Whence did it all come? Simply because the son of a
common laborer, a carpenter, had hung on a cross and
died. The crowned heads of Europe were controlled by
that laborer's spirit of sacrifice and devotion. Germany,
France, Italy and other countries allied themselves and
organized an army many times the size of that of Japan,
while time after time they tried to regain the tiny plot
of ground on which the Tomb is situated.

They did not seek more land but more religion. The
Japanese remember the story of the occupation of Kaga
Province by the Ikko Sect of Buddhism during a period
of ninety-three years. But the Crusaders continued their
effort for more than twice as long and were many times
the size of the forces of Rennyo Shonin, the Ikko leader.

From the modern point of view, the Crusades were a
strange adventure, but their motive was that of sacrificial
service. For the sake of Christ the Crusaders plodded
along on foot from England to France, France to Italy,

thence to Greece and at last to Asia Minor. Consider the depth of feeling which must have inspired them! These were ideal warriors. They would forgive an enemy, if only he would give them leave to worship freely in the holy land of Jesus. They had developed the chivalry which renders merciful service to women and children. It is this chivalry which impresses us in reading the stories of the Crusades. It represents the height of romance. I am against war but I find myself responding to the spirit of the Crusaders.

Once more I ask, whence did it arise? It came from the faith in the heart of that carpenter. He was convinced that for him to endure agony patiently was to become a vicarious sacrifice for the worst sin in the world. The Crusaders were possessed by the same belief. In the spirit of the Cross they died. They sought to protect the banner of the Cross. The Crusaders can be explained only by the Cross.

PRACTISING LOVE, NOT THEORIZING ABOUT IT

Modern Christians are called to be Crusaders also, but on a higher level. Like that crucified carpenter, we must also take upon ourselves the responsibility for our generation. This means not only forgiving the folks who crucify us, but even laying hold of the worst of the sins of modern society and curing them, redeeming them, adjusting them, just as much as if they were our own personal sins that we ourselves had committed. Rejoicing in the incidental sacrifice and suffering, we must reorganize society so as to lift all human beings up to the high places of God. Therefore, as did the Crusaders of old, we choose the Cross as our symbol; for in this definition of it lies the height of morality and the heart of Christianity.

Tolstoi was attracted to Jesus by his teaching of love, and in his turn interpreted it to many others. And yet I feel that Tolstoi never fully understood the very thing which he sought to exemplify, for he maintained that the most extraordinary thing about Jesus was his ideas. " Man is a fool on his instinctive levels," wrote the Russian prophet, " but through ideas he can control his instincts. The reason for the greatness of Jesus was the superiority of his thinking." So far, so good. But must we stop there? I cannot agree with Tolstoi in that the instincts can be controlled by mere ideas. Ideas alone are valueless. Deeds must express them. Tolstoi says the Sermon on the Mount is the great thing, but the actual life of Jesus in which he practised what he preached seems to me greater even than the Sermon on the Mount. Jesus incarnated love in his ideas, but more than that he was the very incarnation of love in his practice.

The idea of love was not new with him, but his consistent practice was. Take, for instance, the matter of non-resistance. Jesus was not the only prophet in his time to teach the love of enemies. In his *History of the Jews*, Josephus tells the story of a contemporary of Jesus who held the same idea and who was also a revolutionary leader. The difference was that he abandoned his principle of non-resistance when the Roman troops came, and protected himself by force! Jesus was unique since because he loved his enemies he offered no resistance and remained silent in the presence of those who dragged him to trial. Today we have forgotten even the name of the other, while we remember the name of Jesus.

The reasons for the arrest of Jesus are clear. In the first place, he was said to be a traitor. Appearances were against him in this regard, for it looked as though he had gathered together five thousand men and plotted an in-

surrection. The truth was, however, that it was not he
who had done the planning, but the gang of five thousand
insurrectionists who had sought to prevail upon him to
fall in with their plot.

In Japan we have a similar story, that of Saigo Taka-
mori, with a very different outcome. Saigo permitted
himself to be forced by his followers to start what is known
in Japanese history as the Saigo Insurrection. They
came to him and said, " Saigo, it is begun. Is it all right? "
In contrast to Jesus' withdrawal from the five thousand,
Saigo answered with a non-committal " Uhuh! " and thus
condemned the country to a ten years' warfare.

Again, Jesus had set aside the religious ceremonialism
of the day and to the police was a disturber of the peace.
He had said, " Destroy this temple! " (John 2:19.) Built
at a cost of two billion yen, this temple was to the Jews
their sacred national shrine, comparable to the Imperial
Shrine of the ancestors of the Japanese Emperors at Ise.
Early in the modern era the Japanese Minister of Education who was famed and feared for his progressiveness,
Yurei Mori, was assassinated for a similar reason. An
unfounded rumor was circulated that he had lifted the
curtain of the holy of holies of this sacred shrine, with
his walking stick.*

One more reason for the arrest of Jesus was that he
had called himself the Son of God, and this was blasphemy.
Treason, disturbing the peace, and blasphemy! Taken
together these three certainly constituted crime worthy
of capital punishment. And the third of these, blasphemy,
is punishable by death in Japan also, only that in our
country it is irreverence toward the Throne instead of
blasphemy toward God.

* At this time in Japan it was profanity to lift the curtain of the
Ise shrine even with one's hand, and much worse to do so with a stick.

Aware of these circumstances, Jesus made a firm resolution to face death and went forward in that decision. His opposition came mostly from the religious leaders of his day. It was the Pharisees, the Mussolin-ists of that time and country, who brought him to his death. This party had six thousand members and was very zealous, and of a narrow, exclusive spirit, like the Nichiren Buddhists of Japan. Jesus was broad-minded and would eat with all sorts of people. " Look at that degenerate fellow! " they would say, " eating with tax-gatherers and sinners! He's unfit to lead the nation! "

The Pharisees were bitterly opposed to paying taxes to their foreign conquerors, the Romans. Jesus offended these rabid nationalists by saying it was all right to do so, and they suspected him of being in cahoots with the bribed government officials, and even of receiving bribes himself. " While we pray and fast for national reconstruction, Jesus eats and drinks and never fasts. He is a godless wretch," they criticized. But those persons were themselves rather soiled with money.

The Sadducees, the ruling class, were the ones who wanted to make money from the religious ceremonials. It had become the rule that a bull could not be offered for sacrifice unless it had been temple-branded. This created a monopoly and a single bull worth six yen was sold in the Temple by the Sadducees for six times that amount, or thirty-six yen. No one was allowed to go outside and bring in other cattle for sacrifice and thus break the monopoly. Christ said that was wrong and drove out the profiteers. At that, strife broke out between the religious leaders and the ruling class, for it became true that with Jesus present these latter could not make their swollen profits. Naturally this was an excellent reason for having him executed.

It was when this issue arose that Jesus said something about destroying the temple. " Why did you overturn the tables and drive out the beasts? " he was asked, and replied, as in John 2:19, " Destroy this temple and in three days I will rebuild it." To the Oriental there is obvious a touch of humor in this cryptic reply. Jesus was humorously looking forward to his own impending demolition, all the more to be expected because of that particular day's work of temple-cleansing.

JESUS IN COURT

As we have said, Jesus was arrested because of the decision of the Sanhedrin of Seventy Elders. The Sanhedrin's order is recorded (John 11:57) to have Jesus arrested as quickly as possible. This order probably looked much like those in north China today, where the visitor finds great gates at the entrance to the walled cities and villages, with placards on the gates reading something as follows:

REWARD OFFERED
TEN THOUSAND PIECES OF GOLD
FOR THE HEAD OF SO-AND-SO

At the village gates in Judea there were probably placards posted reading,

THIRTY PIECES OF SILVER
FOR THE HEAD OF JESUS

and below such words were probably added the reasons he was wanted by the authorities: he was a traitor, a blasphemer, and a law-breaker.

Jesus was arrested in the park of the Mount of Olives, in which the ancient olive trees are still standing. On the way to the Garden of Gethsemane on the north side of Jerusalem there is a bridge, just beyond the Beautiful Gate. Probably they went through the Gate to reach it. Jesus passed the Temple and went out through this Gate on his way to the Garden. Thus he may have been seen by the nationalist leader, Annas, the son-in-law of Caiaphas the chief priest, the president of the senate, whose position was like that of the head of the group of Elder Statesmen of Japan. It was by the servants of Annas that Jesus was arrested.

"You say you have come from heaven — is it true?"

"How about your having said you would destroy the Temple?"

At these questions Jesus was silent. His accusers were offended at his silence and could do nothing, for they had no power to execute capital punishment. So the next day they took him to Pilate. The latter said, "That is not my sort of a problem. That is a religious issue." And because he was of unsound conscience, Pilate evaded the issue by saying, "This case belongs to another jurisdiction. Jesus is a Galilean. Send him to the palace of Herod Antipas."

Christ was sent to Herod, and thus, while being sent from place to place, was convicted as a traitor. Herod was anxious to see Christ face to face. Ever since he had killed John the Baptist, alarmed to the point of seeing John's ghost, Herod had been in fear that Christ was John come to life again.

But though they brought before him this Christ who was John resurrected, Christ was silent and said nothing. He had called Herod a fox. Herod had committed adultery, having married the daughter of King Areta and then divorced her. Christ knew Herod for what he was. So when Herod asked, "Are you intending to stir up a revolution?" Christ said nothing. Herod was nonplussed and said, " This does not belong to my jurisdiction," and sent him back to Pilate.

Johanna, the wife of Chusa, Herod's minister, was intimate with the wife of Pilate. It appears that these two women had some conversation about Christ about this time, for Pilate's wife said to her husband: " That Jesus Christ is a greater man even than John, and it would be very wrong to kill him. I have been warned in a dream."

Now Pilate's wife was the niece of Tiberias Caesar. Pilate was not made governor of Syria because he was great himself, but because of his wife. So when his wife said he ought not to do anything, Pilate should have heeded her. That is written in the Bible. Therefore Pilate washed his hands before the crowd and said, " I will have nothing to do with this affair." But when the crowd got angry and demanded, " What! Won't you judge a man who is against Caesar? " Pilate was disturbed and uncertain as to what to do in the face of this challenge. He probably walked back and forth, back and forth, in indecision, in and out of the court. And finally he said, " All right! " and rendered judgment that Christ was to be executed.

Pilate had two or three passages of dialogue with Christ: " It is true that you say you are the King of the Jews? " " Yes, it is true! "

Christ was not talking about an earthly kingdom, and Pilate knew it. He knew that Christ was speaking religiously in calling himself a king. But after their conversation was over, Pilate was forced by the crowd to deliver Christ up to be executed. The details of Christ's trial are described in Matthew.

CHRIST ON THE CROSS

Christ was taken to Mount Calvary outside the city of Jerusalem, and crucified on the top of this hill. He lived while hanging on the Cross from nine in the morning until about three in the afternoon.

Crucifixion is the most severe form of capital punishment. Executions at the time of the Tokugawa Shogunate took the form of decapitation after *harakiri,* a much less cruel form of punishment. It was the Romans who invented crucifixion. Crucifixion does not affect the heart nor cut the arteries. The person is simply hung up by nails. Death comes as a result of nervous exhaustion, by starvation, or by bleeding. In Japan, although crucifixion was used as a form of punishment, they used to mitigate the cruelty of it by killing those who were to be executed by shooting them with arrows after they were put on the cross.

There were two others crucified with Christ. On each side of him was a robber.

There are seven famous Words which Christ cried out on the cross.

I. The first was: " Father, forgive them, for they know not what they do." Ordinary human beings are likely to say, rather, " Remember it against them! " It was just at that point that Christ was unique, in that he forgave people and did not think evil of them. At whatever point we tap it, Christ's story is a story of love.

Yukinaga Konishi,* a Japanese Catholic Christian of

* French and Spanish friars brought Christianity to Japan in the seventeenth century. After many had been converted the government took alarm from these words of a shipwrecked Spanish captain: " After the priests will come my King and his soldiers and take your country." Thousands of Christians were martyred, and their blood has become the seed of the Japanese church today.

three centuries ago, was crucified in the Sanjo river bed at
Kyoto, and because he remained silent at the time of his
dying, he is a great man in Western (Catholic) history,
though in Japanese history he is written of merely as a
worthless fellow who had embraced Christianity. He was
really a very great person. One of his friends was Haramondo, a relative of Kasuga no Tsubone, who is said to
have lived at Kasuga Cho, Koishikawa, Tokyo, where the
Suda eye hospital now stands. Haramondo sympathized
with Yukinaga Konishi and advised the latter to give up
his Christianity, but he would not listen, and so was finally
crucified. Haramondo is written of in the *Dai Bosatsu
Toke,* under the title of " Adoration of the Holy Mother,"
by Nakazato Kaizan.

From the point of view of human instincts, enemies are
to be hated, but Christ could forgive them. Love must go
as far as this. And this becomes possible as the Spirit of
God enters a man. As a mother loves her erring child, we
must love our enemies and pray God for their forgiveness.
Apart from God this spirit of forgiving enemies is not com-
prehensible. When a woman has been married and then
divorced, if she lacks faith, she feels resentful, but with
religious faith she can have the spirit of " Father, forgive
them."

II. " Today thou shalt be with me in Paradise." This
is Christ's second saying on the Cross.

One of the two robbers, probably the one being crucified
on the left, called insultingly to him: " Hey, Jesus, if ye're
the Son of God, hadn't y'oughter save us as well as yer-
self? "

Hearing that, the robber on the right began to speak in
defense of Christ: " Hey, you fellow there, there's a world
of difference between this honorable gentleman and yourself. This gentleman has done no wrong."

And then he asked of Christ: " Sir, when you go to Heaven, please remember me." At once Christ answered: "All right! Today you will be with me in Paradise."

Thus, even in his last hour, Christ gave the poor fellow the assurance that he could go to heaven. At such a time, when he was in intolerable pain, it would have been entirely excusable in him to have put off such a request from another person by saying that he could not pay attention to it, and to ask him to wait till a more convenient occasion. But Christ, because from the bottom of his heart he wanted to save men, revealed his will-to-save them even in his last moment.

As for me, I am ashamed to say that when the unemployed come in great numbers, I get tired out and finally am likely to say unkind things to them. Shopkeepers, too, when they are busy or absorbed in their own affairs are likely to become angry at the telephone interruptions. But Christ did nothing of the kind.

III. Christ, anxious about his mother, and seeing her and his beloved disciple standing near one another, said to her, " Woman behold thy son," and to his disciple, " Behold thy mother."

IV. He said, " I thirst." At that, those who were standing beside the cross tried to get him to drink a narcotic. Ordinarily, when suffering such excruciating pain, anyone would have wanted to be put out of misery as soon as possible. But Christ refused the drug and died in full consciousness.

V. He cried, " *Eli, Eli, lama, sabachtani*," which means, " My God, my God, why hast thou forsaken me? " People who hate Christianity say that for Christ to say this in his dying moment was cowardly. Kato Hiroyuki criticized this as a cowardly expression, but Christ was quoting the first verse of Psalm Twenty-two. Sung hundreds of years beforehand, this Twenty-second Psalm is prophetic of a righteous person suffering on the Cross, and of the casting of lots even for his clothing. Christ, seeing before his very eyes the casting of lots for his clothing, was reminded of this Psalm, and sang it with a loud voice.

VI. If this interpretation of the Fifth Word were incorrect, the Sixth Word, " It is finished," would not have been uttered. For just *what* was finished? It was the work of redeeming mankind that was finished. Christ endured up to this point.

VII. His last word was " Father, into thy hands I commit my spirit." Saying this, he ceased to breathe. Christ did not use the cold word, " God," but said " Father." And he spoke not of death but rather said, " Take charge of my spirit." The message for us in this utterance of Christ is very clear. Just as we ask the bank to take care of our money, we are to ask God to care for our souls. If in our self-will we keep hold of them ourselves, we are likely to do them grave injury; but if we commit them to God, they are safe.

Thus the first and the last of the Seven Words on the Cross are prayers.

AN ANALYSIS OF THE CROSS-CONSCIOUSNESS

Then why did Christ die? This is a question about which, as has been said before, misunderstanding often arises. We take it for granted that Christ was Christ from the beginning, but that was not the case. His first name was Jesus. " Christ " is a name given him afterward as a title of reverence. While he was alive, Christ did not think of himself as great or extraordinary. When the disciples said, " You are the Son of God," Christ humbly told them to keep silent. And they were told that if they believed in him they would be able to do " greater things " than he did.

Since Christ was a humble-minded person, he himself never said he was the Christ, even though he was told, " You are the Son of God." When John the Baptist sent messengers and asked him, " Are you the One the Jewish people have long been awaiting? " these messengers received the answer, " The blind receive their sight, the lame walk, the lepers are cleansed, the deaf hear, the dead are raised, the poor have the gospel preached to them; and blessed is he, whosoever finds no occasion of stumbling in me."

Religion is the creation of values. It is making worthless people over into worthy ones. Real Christianity consists, not in handsome placards before church edifices, but in tearing down such signs if need be, in order to be able to win and save even one victim of unemployment.

The name, Christ, was given later. Peter used it first of all. Even though there are folks who talk continually about Christ's second coming, it will not do to believe them; their emphasis is a mistaken one.* The real Christ is one who dies for others.

To love men to the uttermost — that is what Christ does. To that end, sin must be redeemed. Simply to be inactive and not to commit sin one's self is not enough. Next door is a slum, and in it there are prostitutes and unemployed, living in the crowded housing of slum con-

---

* " In the Japanese Holiness church and in the Free Methodist Church in Japan they have a peculiar psychology. They say that Christ is coming on the top of Mt. Fuji, and they are preparing white robes to wear when they shall meet him there. They have fixed the month, year, and even the day of his appearance, calculating it from the Book of Daniel. They are too much in a hurry!" (Quotation from one of Dr. Kagawa's addresses in Shanghai, in the Shanghai Number, *Friends of Jesus*.)

ditions. To turn blind eyes and deaf ears toward these —
this is sin! Christ was fully conscious of such conditions,
he thought as God does about them, he suffered profoundly in his soul about them, and so was put on the
Cross and died.

Among the slum-dwellers I have known there have been
many murderers — some even among my former Sunday
School children — but those who had some Christian
teaching agonized over their sins. One of these was
Fujita Sanzo, a bean-curd seller. One day Fujita killed
a drunken man accidentally, by striking him in anger
when the drunk overturned and ruined his day's supply
of precious bean curd. After that Fujita was tormented
by the ghost of the dead man. Fujita came to me and
said, " God is with you, and if I may take hold of your
hand when I go to sleep, the ghost will not come." So
after that, every night, he slept with me, holding my hand.
While he continued to hold my hand, the ghost did not
come, but if he was separated from me for even a moment
he would begin to groan.

If the consciousness of sin becomes strong in us, we can
understand that Christ died for us. If your little finger is
wounded, the next finger cannot remain unaffected. If
anyone is struck down by an automobile, the bystanders
who failed to warn cannot disclaim responsibility. Similarly, a textile workers' strike has a profound relationship
to the rest of us. While so many remain unemployed, we
ought all at least to remember them in our prayers, and
give up one meal to help feed them. So long as our
thoughts are partial, biased, and shut up in a class-limited
compartment, we may have no sense of guilt about such
matters; but as soon as we begin to think in universal
terms, we realize that we dare not ignore them, that there
is sin involved in such ignorance. We must shed our

blood in remedying such situations. That is why Christ
said, " My blood is shed for the redemption of sin."

REDEMPTION THE CONSUMMATION OF LOVE

As I said before, man's consciousness may be divided
into three stages — unconsciousness, semi-consciousness,
and full consciousness. In the unconscious stage, men
kill other human beings without thinking anything of it.
In war they kill men and shout, " Banzai! Hurrah! "
But there is something the matter with the man who can
do this. He is still in the unconscious stage.

When semi-consciousness arrives, as it did suddenly
to Naozane Kumagai, he was smitten with the conviction
that he had committed a sin in killing a man, and so became a priest for the rest of his life.* Among the Jews
in the semi-conscious stage, they felt that they could not
die themselves and went no farther than to get a goat to
sacrifice in their place. It would seem very strange to us
today to behave in this manner, but that was the way they
met the situation of sin in ancient times. For eight days
from the tenth of July onward there was always a great
festival in Palestine, to beg God's forgiveness. At that
time a red cloth would be put on the horns of a goat, and
the priest would lay his hand on the goat's head and pray,
(on behalf of all the people) — " Forgive all our sins,
known and unknown, for the past year." According to
Jewish custom, the goat which was to bear the sins of the
people was driven into the wilderness. This was something like the Bon festival of the Japanese people.

When full consciousness comes, a goat is seen to be
insufficient. Saying that he must take the place of the
goat, Christ gave his own life in sacrifice. Unless he

* Naozane Kumagai was an ancient Japanese warrior who killed the
young son of his friend in battle.

offered himself for the sins of others, he would not be worthy to be called the Christ, he thought. And when he was put on the Cross, he said, " It is finished," that is, " It is fulfilled." Herein lies the Christ-like character of Christ. We ordinary folks are very flighty and uncertain, very likely not to carry out our best intentions. But Christ from the beginning planned to die for men, and went straight ahead courageously to carry out that plan.

Christ went steadily forward, with God-consciousness, and endured even the hateful sin of his enemies. The Cross is the consummate crystallization of love. This we reverence; this we call redemptive love. Redemptive love redeems and makes up for the sins of others. Through this redemptive love the people of the world have been saved — no one knows how many billions of them. Human history was at first unconscious; then, up to the time of Christ there was the epoch of semi-consciousness; and since Christ the human race is very gradually becoming fully conscious. But some people do not develop fully, and stop at semi-consciousness.

In social reconstruction this redemptive consciousness is imperative. Even in the creation of a political party, it is necessary that one be lenient with the faults of enemies. Any other attitude in meeting such faults is bound to cause factions in the organization.

Christ set about solving this difficult problem. Therefore Christ's movement is called a Love-Movement.

Without the Cross, the universe does not evolve. Since a sin in any part of society affects the whole, someone must assume responsibility for the whole. Therefore, unless the Cross-consciousness is reflected in us, we cannot bring about real social reconstruction. Therein lies the truth of the Eternal Cross. This is why over a period of two hundred years, hundreds of thousands of people attempted to regain the tomb of Christ.

I repeat it — unless someone becomes a stepping stone for others, society will not improve. The proletarian parties split up because they lacked the spirit of service for others. On the other hand, if one aims, in any situation, to become a *sacrifice* for others, victory is near. And if we can progressively develop this spirit of sacrifice within ourselves, the world is bound to get better.

Everywhere the world is waiting for those who will sacrifice themselves for others — in the villages, in the towns, in the factories, the schools, the hospitals. For anyone who aspires to be a leader, it is absolutely necessary to have this spirit of Christ. Lenin spoke of being under the banner of Marx, but I want to challenge men everywhere to foregather under the banner of the Cross of Christ.

PRAYER

Father God: When we meditate on the road trodden by Jesus the Carpenter, it is of the blood of the Cross which he shed that we think, and give thanks. Nevertheless even yet we do not understand this Blood of Christ. Though even yet we may be doubting it as an historical fact, we thank Thee that Christ did indeed reveal the spirit of God on earth, for our Salvation. We are gathered here together under the banner of the Cross, repenting of our sins, and for the salvation of others. Enable us to pass our whole lives in the spirit of the Cross, participating in the suffering of God, and sharing in His Love, to lift the world and save it, carrying it on our shoulders. Through Christ we pray. Amen.

III

THE CROSS IN THE MIND OF CHRIST

Blessed are they which are persecuted for righteousness' sake: for theirs is the kingdom of heaven.

Blessed are ye when men shall revile you, and persecute you, and shall say all manner of evil against you falsely, for my sake. Matthew 5:10, 11.

THE WORDS printed above from Matthew's Gospel are the first words of Jesus in which a shadow appears. Even as early as this, Jesus had made up his mind that the Righteous One must suffer. Thus his crucifixion was anticipated by him very early; it was not something accepted somewhere in the course of his later experience. The more profound and penetrating his understanding of life became, the more the Cross was stamped upon his bosom. In Matthew 9:15, he says that the Bridegroom, Christ, will be taken captive by the people. This was in the early days of the Galilean ministry and I think it had some relation to the imprisonment of John the Baptist.

In the mind of Jesus there was the thought that the righteous person must suffer. Unless the righteous one suffered, he could not be called a righteous person. The pastors and evangelists of both Christianity and Buddhism lose their mission when they live too comfortably. Anyone who aims at accomplishment must expect to meet with opposition.

Next, Jesus is shown saying the same thing in his teaching to the disciples. In Matthew 10:17–23 he is telling them that they will meet with persecutions and giving them the courage to face them. How is it with us? We who have resolved to take up our cross and live in austerity — have we the courage to fight for righteousness as wholeheartedly as Christ did? We ought not to expect to live in comfort. We must rise above the evils of society, convinced that Jesus is always at our side, saying to us, " Yes, of course you are going to be persecuted for My Sake; are you ready for it? "

In Matthew 10:38–39 the word "cross" appears for the first time. Just what does it mean here? " And he that taketh not his cross, and followeth not after me, is not worthy of me. He that findeth his life shall lose it: and he that loseth his life for my sake shall find it." This is a paradox. All religious truth is, I believe, ultimately paradox. That which is nothing to us is perfect to God, and all our perfection that we gain with so much effort is as nothing to him.

In Kobe, a young man once came to me and said he wanted to be an evangelist.

" Have you the courage to go to prison? " I asked him. " Have you the grit to lead a strike? "

" No," he answered.

" Then give up the idea of becoming an evangelist," I said.

The kind of Christianity which makes me want to save myself alone is useless. We must lay hold upon a more ardent, fervent, passionate faith.

THE ANNOUNCEMENT OF THE CROSS

Then Jesus thought more and more deeply. Even at the time of the Galilean ministry, he was meditating profoundly upon the Cross. Thus he began to realize that he must finally face toward his goal of crucifixion. We may think that Jesus did not begin to be aware of the likelihood of crucifixion until after John's execution, but according to Matthew this is not the case. Even in the midst of the Galilean ministry, he is already conscious of the Cross: " But he answered and said unto them, An evil and adulterous generation seeketh after a sign; and there shall no sign be given to it, but the sign of the prophet Jonas. For as Jonas was three days and three nights in the whale's belly, so shall the Son of Man be three days and three nights in the heart of the earth."

In Matthew 12:40 Jesus says, " The Son of Man must be three days and nights in the heart of the earth." This Cross-consciousness develops at the very height of Christ's popularity during the Galilean ministry. For when he said that the real sign which he would give would be that of Jonah, who was immured in the stomach of a fish, it shows that he was already aware that he would meet with capital punishment in some form. To be three days and nights in the stomach of a fish signified the Cross. Thus Jesus hinted at the Cross at this time, but this made no impression on the minds of the disciples. But when we reach the 16th chapter of Matthew, we notice that the situation is changed. In Matthew 16:21 occur the words: " He began to show them." And from this time on Jesus says clearly that he must be killed at Jerusalem. Those who are to kill him are the priests, the scholars, and the king; and he is the one who is to be killed and is to be put on the cross and to be resurrected on the third day. This had been implied when he mentioned Jonah. This consciousness of Jesus became a vivid reality, a new point of departure. A great religious leader of England, J. Campbell Morgan, has called this moment when he began to teach the cross openly, the crisis of Christ.

A great many people are not willing to accept literally this dark cross teaching. Nineteenth century theology did not understand this thing called the Cross. During the nineteenth century, the opinion prevailed that the cross was unimportant, but I think that the Cross is Jesus' central idea. Why did he speak of it? There are three reasons.

THE THREE REASONS

First, without the Cross, Jesus thought that he could not make his point clear. The environment probably forced him to the Cross. During that cruel Roman era one's message would hardly carry weight unless one were crucified. At present there is such a general acceptance of Christianity that the Department of Education helps to distribute Christian posters, and we are all apt to be too easy-going. But Jesus could not ascend to the right hand of the Father without having first endured the cross.

The second reason was neither related to the social environment nor to the idea of Jesus; rather, it was because it was written in the scriptures. These, to a great extent, guided the mind of Jesus. In Mark 9:12 it says: " Elijah does indeed come first and reforms everything, and do not the scriptures say of the Son of Man that he will suffer much and be refused? " It is as if he were asking: " Say, you disciples of mine, what do you think the Bible means when it says that the Savior who is called the Son of Man will come, and that this Savior must undergo much suffering? " This described Christ's own feelings, his attitude toward life.

And we too, how do we interpret this passage? In Psalms 22 and Isaiah 53, it is written that the Son of Man is not to have merely glory and success but that he must inevitably undergo suffering. And Jesus is saying to us, " Say, how do you read that passage? What does it mean to *you?* " If Christ possessed the consciousness of being the Son of Man, the Savior, it was also necessary for him to have the consciousness of the Cross.

Jesus gave an ambiguous answer to the question of John the Baptist in Matthew 11:26. When asked, " Art thou he that cometh? " Christ did not reply, " Yes," for he knew that " he that cometh " — he for whom John and all the Jews were waiting — must be put on a cross. Jesus thought that he was the One who was to come but he had not yet brought that to realization by being put on the Cross. I think this was Jesus' honest self-criticism in view of the fact that the Cross-announcement of his Messiahship was as yet a matter of the future.

Jesus was not at that time yet revealed as the " Suffering Messiah." So although he himself possessed the Messianic consciousness, a Christ-with-a-good-reputation, such as he had at that time, was not yet a real Messiah. A real Messiah must go through more suffering, he thought. The suffering Christ comes first, the glorified one afterward. The Messiah the disciples were thinking of was a Messiah of glory only, but the one that he himself was thinking of was a Christ who entered into his glory after passing through suffering, who came to resurrection after enduring the Cross. He thought the two things went together in an inevitable sequence. We need to enter more deeply into this central idea of his.

POINTING TOWARD THE CROSS

Having thus broached the subject, Jesus frequently came back to it, especially on the way home from his second journey to foreign parts. " Then said Jesus unto his disciples, If any man will come after me, let him deny himself, and take up his cross and follow me." (Matt. 16:24.)

At the end of the 10th chapter of Matthew, he repeats the same thing. Here, however, Jesus is still vague and indefinite, but when we reach the 16th of Matthew, he says it clearly: " Let each one take up his cross and follow me." The position of these words is not accidental. The ambiguity with which Jesus at first held obscurely that the righteous would experience suffering such as that of Jonah has here given place to the clear statement that he is to die.

Jesus' first thought of the Cross grew out of his realization of the social circumstances in which he found himself; second, from his conception of sacrifice as revealed in the scriptures; and third, from his inner sense of his responsibility to God and humanity. After he had said, as in Matthew 16:24, " You also must bear the cross," Jesus climbed a mountain and when he came down from the mountain, he quoted scripture:

" And as they came down from the mountain, Jesus charged them saying, ' Tell the vision to no man, until the Son of Man be risen again from the dead.'

" And his disciples asked him, saying, ' Why then say the scribes that Elias must first come? '

" And Jesus answered and said unto them, ' Elias truly shall first come, and restore all things.'

" But I say unto you, ' That Elias is come already, and they knew him not, but have done unto him whatsoever they listed. Likewise shall also the Son of Man suffer of them.'

" Then the disciples understood that he spake unto them of John the Baptist." (Matt. 17:9-13.)

The Cross spoken of in the scriptures, Jesus here says, is the same as the Cross he must bear. Matthew 17:9 which speaks of Elijah, mentions him thus the second time.

Here once more Jesus repeats that he is to suffer. From that time, after descending the mountain, Jesus faces steadily down toward the dark way of the cross. Reaching the bottom of the mountain he says, in Matthew 17:17, "How long shall I be with you!" At this time a dark premonition comes to him that his time is short. And in Matthew 17:22–23 it is recorded that in returning from the second evangelistic journey he said, "I am to be killed," and that the disciples were sorrowful.

After this, Jesus becomes more and more explicit in the expression of his deep conviction. The disciples gaze at him in amazement as he hastens forward. And although he is on his way toward Jerusalem, Jesus says clearly, "I am to be put on the cross." This he repeats in Matthew 26, on the night that they eat the Last Supper. His being put on the cross is for the shedding of blood, the remission of sins as it is written in the scripture, " I must shed my blood." In this fashion Jesus, convinced that he is to shed his blood for the human race, shows his determination to accept whatever happens, and yet prays: " If it be possible, take this cup from me."

THE HOLY AGONY

Although from the starting point in the fifth chapter of Matthew Jesus was resolved to face death, as he approached the end of his life, he suffered agony. Some may call this cowardly and say that when he was agonizing and suffering about his death he showed himself a desperate man. " If it be possible, let this cup pass from me." Though they may call this the utterance of a coward, I think that without the record of this agony, the story would have been false to human nature. To be determined up to this point to say he would give his whole life to God and yet, when he faced the scaffold, to say:

" Yes, I will submit to death as God's lamb, but if it be possible, please take this cup from me," — this I believe to be genuine. This is a real human Jesus. Though he may seem weak who says: " I am continually thinking that I must become a substitute and die for men, and if the human race needs such a sacrifice, O God, please let it take place." But the modernists say, " If God is love, such a sacrifice ought not to be needed." I believe, however, that this prayer of Christ's was sincere, and at the last, when his prayer was not heard, God did demand the blood of redemption, and Jesus said: " Thy will be done. If you need my life, I offer it up." The very night when he prayed in this way, Jesus was arrested.

This was the Cross which emerged out of the three-year-long process of Jesus' thought, the Cross-consciousness that developed through the working of his mental processes. At first Jesus seems to have thought the Cross was necessary more as a teaching of the truth, but along about the middle of his ministry, meditating on the death of John, on the predicted death of the Son of Man, and on all suffering in general, he suggested to his disciples that he must be killed. He discusses the same question in the Gethsemane prayer: " If God's love can be brought fully into operation without my passing through suffering, please save me. But I will not insist upon my own desires." Thus saying, Jesus gladly embraced the Cross.

How is it with us? Do we have this same thoroughgoing point of view? The Cross is our Cross. We must not think of it merely as a metaphor. We ourselves must be ready to be put on the Cross. Not seeking a success-Christ, we must more and more profoundly contemplate the Christ who accepted suffering and endured agony up to the final moment of the Cross.

PRAYER

Father God: Even today we are still absorbed in the contemplation of the Figure of Christ, as he suffered and agonized from the peak of popularity during the Galilean ministry to the time of his elevation on the Cross. But we ourselves, we confess it with shame, are always choosing things which are selfish, comfortable, too much according to our own preferences and tastes. Show us, we beseech thee, the way of the Cross that we must follow, the way of Jesus. Show to me, I pray thee, the Cross in my daily occupation, the Cross in my intellectual life, the Cross connected with my economic status, the Cross in my social life, the Cross in my family life, and the Cross that I must bear for Jesus' sake. Even though I shrink back from the Cross and say as Jesus said, " If possible do not put this cross upon me, if possible take this cup away from me," yet if this Cross and this cup be mine to bear and drink, enable me to accept them gladly. In ever deeper meditation on the Cross, enable each one of us to become a lesser Christ and to bring his truth into active and effective operation in this present day world. In his Holy Name, we pray. Amen.

IV

THE CROSS IN THE FOURTH GOSPEL

The bread that I will give for the world's life is my own flesh. John 6:51.

WE ARE all taught to connect Christianity with the Cross. Even outside the Christian community, the Cross is constantly mentioned. The Cross means sacrifice, and a brave, gallant spirit of rising above suffering. No one has yet learned enough about how to put that Cross into practice. Therefore let us ask the Fourth Gospel to yield us its secret.

There are four books in the New Testament which are biographies of Jesus Christ — Matthew, Mark, Luke and John. Of these, Matthew, Mark and Luke are similar and are called the Synoptic Gospels, while the Fourth Gospel is different from the others. There seems to be a reason for this dissimilarity. It may have been because the disciples had arranged and agreed among themselves that the author of the Fourth Gospel should record the things that are not written in Matthew, Mark or Luke. After the death of Jesus, they knew there would be a new era, that the age would change, and it did change. There would be no one else to record it, so they may have agreed to ask this writer of the Fourth Gospel to do so.

Differing thus from the three Synoptics, the Fourth Gospel is a most interesting record. Its materials are probably derived not so much from the common people as in the cases of Matthew, Mark and Luke, but rather

from the court, the governmental authorities. Thus we get
the story told from a different angle. In studying the story
of Kotoku Denjiro,* if one takes only what his friends
said about him, the account is biassed, partial, one-sided.
But if one takes the testimony of the government officials
who examined him, there is a different side of the tale.

Whether John wrote or did not write the Gospel which
bears his name, it does carry strong evidence that much
of its material came from government authorities. Among
these officials were those who reverenced Jesus, such as
Nicodemus, and Joseph of Arimathea. Though openly
the latter did not ally himself with Christ, he may secretly
have had communication with him; at any rate we know
that Christ was buried in his tomb.† Both Joseph and
Nicodemus were members of the Sanhedrin which conducted the first trial of Jesus.

There was still another prominent official named Chusa,
who was not a Roman but one of the lords associated with
the King of Judea. Chusa is mentioned first among the

* The name of Kotoku Denjiro is a by-word in Japan as that of the
most famous would-be assassin of a Japanese Emperor. In the early
years of this century, socialistic ideas were developing in Tokyo, especially in the forum which took the place of a Sunday service at the
Unitarian church. There were two parties. One believed in evolutionary
and the other in revolutionary methods. The evolutionists eventuated
in the Japan Federation of Labor, which now owns the old Unitarian
church buildings as its headquarters. The revolutionists, led by Kotoku,
left the church and, it is alleged, hatched a plan to assassinate the Emperor. Kotoku and a dozen others were executed before any overt acts
had been perpetrated. But the popular reaction against radicalism was
so severe as to retard for years the efforts of social workers. It is said
that the police confiscated from a mission school library even a book on
The Social Life of Ants!

† In Palestine there was a custom of borrowing a tomb for a person
recently deceased, and of keeping the body in the borrowed tomb for
about three months, surrounded by obituary gifts, before its final disposition. The person who lent his tomb to Christ was Joseph of
Arimathea.

members of the official class who came in contact with
Jesus, in the Fourth Gospel, the circumstance being that
his son was healed of illness by Jesus, and because of this
healing of the child's illness Chusa's wife, Johanna, went
about serving Jesus. (John 4.)

Since the materials in the Fourth Gospel probably came
from such sources, we may expect to have the governmental side emphasized. For instance, in John 7:44 it is
recorded that officers were sent to arrest Jesus, but that
these officers joined with the multitude in admiration of
him. Again John 11:47-53 leaves no room for doubt that
it was Sanhedrin members themselves who furnished some
of the materials in John's Gospel. For there it is written
in detail, that on the very day the Sanhedrin convened, it
was decided to have Jesus executed; and that the order
was sent out as recorded in John 11:57: "For the high
priests and the Pharisees had given orders that anyone
who found out where he was should let them know, so that
they might arrest him."

Although in this fashion the decision of the Sanhedrin
to kill Jesus had probably been published at the street
corners of the towns and villages of the region, this Sanhedrin decision did not by any means represent a unani-
mous opinion among its own members. It was like the
way things go in the Tokyo City Assembly, where the pro-
nouncements of one or two influential men decide the pattern of events. There was a significant minority in the
Sanhedrin which approved of Jesus, but was not able to
confess it, because of fear for their own reputations:
"Even among the leading men, many came to believe in
him, but on account of the Pharisees they would not acknowledge it, for fear of being excluded from the syna-
gogues, for they cared more for the approval of men than
for the approval of God." (John 12:42-43.)

The Fourth Gospel is undoubtedly composed of records contributed by those who possessed an intimate knowledge of the inside facts about the Jewish government. In fact, these men who contributed to these materials were already repenting of their share in having killed Jesus and of the whole occurrence. That is why even the things which Pilate said confidentially to the tribunal are written up, for instance, what he said concerning the placard put over Jesus' head on the cross:

> "Pilate had written a placard and had it put on the cross; it read 'Jesus the Nazarene, the king of the Jews.' Many of the Jews read this placard, for the place where Jesus was crucified was near the city, and it was written in Hebrew, Latin, and Greek. So the Jewish high priests said to Pilate,
> "Do not write, 'The king of the Jews,' but write, He said, 'I am the king of the Jews.'"
> Pilate answered,
> "What I have written, I have written!" (John 19:19-22.)

This record of the parley between the Sanhedrin and the governor could hardly have been written except by an intimate observer of the governmental situation, someone who had freedom to go and come continually at the court.

The Fourth Gospel is therefore a record of the impression made by Jesus on the Jerusalem officials. It was no doubt Nicodemus, who figures in chapter three, and Chusa, whose son was healed in chapter four, who, being members of the company which put Jesus to death, made their confessions to his most beloved disciples:

"It was like this . . ."

"That was the way it happened . . ."

"Really I don't know how to express my intolerable regret . . ."

In some such fashion, at the annual memorial days, year by year, they may have recalled and repented of it.

Written under such circumstances, the Fourth Gospel is
a reliable document. In the three Synoptics the reasons
for Jesus' execution are not clearly set forth. It is evident
from them merely that a person who did not deserve death
met with capital punishment. Only in the Fourth Gospel
are the reasons given for this tragedy.

In 1919 I wrote a book called "Adoration of the Laborer" and was haled to court for it, for the first time in
my experience. The court records on this occasion read
as follows: "Although he appears moderate, temperate
and sound, he is really crafty, sly, subtle, insidious, de-
signing, treacherous and double-faced; and through advancing radical theories gives the impression of cherishing
revolutionary ideas! "

In the Fourth Gospel there are passages which read
similarly. To the eyes of the officials of that time Jesus
seemed a dangerous person, but when they came to think
it over afterwards, those same men probably said to themselves: "Confound it all! I made a bad mistake! When
I ought to have been helping him! . . . Now I will get to
work and think through this new thing called Christianity! "

At the beginning of the Synoptics one knows that Jesus
is with John the Baptist, but they mention this preparatory period only briefly. "Now after John was delivered
up," (Mark 1:14) makes the life of Jesus begin from that
point. We know, however, that even before that time
there was a preparatory period when Jesus was working
with John the Baptist, and this is written about in the
Fourth Gospel.

Next there is the Galilean period. In this Galilean ministry also, concerning events that Mark mentions but
briefly, the Fourth Gospel inserts, from time to time, accounts of round-trips which Jesus made to Jerusalem. In

the first section of the Galilean ministry Jesus is working alone, while in the second he is surrounded by the disciples, and in the third, by the multitude. Next came Jesus' period of retirement, which began with the death of John. The Fourth Gospel is not clear about this period, but at least one knows from it that there was a reason for such a retirement.

Then comes the period of Perean evangelism, which is fully written up in Luke. After that Jesus went to Jerusalem. About the Jerusalem happenings, it is the Fourth Gospel which goes into most detail. And it records also what the other Gospels do not, namely, that Jesus during his period of retirement was in Samaria. Therefore, though according to the Synoptics the life of Jesus divides into five periods — the Preparation, the Galilean, the Retirement, the Perean and the Jerusalem periods — the Fourth Gospel has this additional Samaritan material.

The Fourth Gospel makes Jerusalem the center and writes of the adverse tide in the period when the opposition to Jesus became intense — of the time when the tornado broke against him — up to the time of the Cross. The counter-currents of this period are not clearly described in the Synoptics but are dramatically set forth in the Fourth Gospel. In John 5:18 the Jews came to the point of thinking that they would kill Jesus. This 18th verse marks the inception of the plan to kill him which developed in Jerusalem.

The situation gradually gets worse until in the sixth chapter John the Baptist is killed, and the reader knows that there are many who are trying to stir up a revolution. The disciples and the multitude get excited and come after Jesus to the number of five thousand. Neither Matthew nor Mark are clear about what follows, recording merely that after John was killed, Jesus retired to the mountains.

The Fourth Gospel tells the story that a great number of people came seeking to stir up a revolution. But Jesus taught them not to seek a revolution against Rome, but a high type of moral revolution. " Jesus, seeing they meant to come and carry him off to make him king, retired again to the hill by himself." (John 6:15.)

When the crowd came to him, Jesus said to them, " The thing you fellows are looking for is an independence movement, but my kind of movement is a different thing." Then, too, it would have been a grave mistake to have attempted to start a revolution with only five thousand mustered. In Acts 5:32 it says that revolts had been planned more than once before; that Theudas had started one which had failed and that later, at the time of the second census, (Luke's second chapter records the first census) Judas of Galilee had started one. This was at a time when Jesus was about ten years of age. So when Jesus came to prominence, the people remembered that earlier movement and came together again; but Jesus refused to have a revolution by violence, and worked wholly for a spiritual movement. Jesus' movement took four hundred years to win through to victory but finally did conquer the Roman empire.

If, at the time of John's death, Jesus had joined with the crowd in a violent revolution, he would probably have been unable to conquer the Roman empire. But in the time of Leo the First, Rome came under the spiritual control of Jesus' movement. At that earlier time, the crowd could not understand this. When they knew that Jesus would not start a revolution, they exclaimed that such a fellow, who lacked love for his country and independence of spirit, was worthless, and left him. " In consequence of this many of his disciples drew back and would not go about with him any longer." (John 6:66.) Jesus had said to John and the other disciples, "Will ye also go away?" Meanwhile the enmity of the crowd toward him was growing.

In the 19th and following verses of the seventh chapter, when Jesus says, "Why are you seeking to kill me?" the reply, "Thou art possessed of a devil — you are crazy," shows that the reputation of Jesus is growing worse and worse. "That fellow is a half-breed — half Jew, half Samaritan — a betrayer, a traitor to his country!" The style and plan of the writing of the other Gospels exclude such materials, but they are naturally central in the dramatic composition of the Fourth Gospel.

There is no mention in the Synoptics, for instance, of the incident described from John 7:30 onward; of the temple attendants' being sent to arrest Jesus and of their being impressed by his words to the extent of forgetting their errand. When they bring back the word recorded in verse 46, "Never man spake as this man," the Pharisees respond, "Have you fellows also been led astray by that creature?" and at that the seventh chapter of John comes to an end, with the man called Nicodemus approving and praising Christ.

In the eighth chapter Jesus is once more speaking at Jerusalem. When he says, "I know that you are descended from Abraham, yet you want to kill me because there is no room in your hearts for my teaching," he is speaking of the plan to kill him to which he refers also in the 28th verse. Thus the purpose to kill Christ is becoming stronger, and the discussion at Jerusalem continues into the eighth chapter.

"You are a Jew, you are possessed of a devil," they say to Christ. And Jesus denies it. And in John 8:58 they take up stones to throw at him, and he goes out of the temple. When things get to such a pass, it is not only the Pharisees but the people also who are against Jesus. Perhaps the people's opposition was because Jesus was too pure, too good for them, so that they could no longer feel comfortable in doing their business in the old ways. Anyway, they, too, were finally in a mood to do away with him.

In the tenth chapter the purpose or conspiracy against Jesus is seen more and more clearly: " The Jews again picked up stones to stone him with. Jesus answered, ' I have let you see many good things from the Father. Which of them do you mean to stone me for? ' The Jews answered, ' We are not stoning you for doing anything good, but for your impious talk, and because you, a mere man, make yourself out to be God.' " And once more they tried there to arrest Jesus. (John 10:39.) And he withdrew out of their reach.

Next, the chief priests and the Pharisees called a meeting of the Sanhedrin, saying they could no longer endure this Jesus' making himself not only a son of God but God himself, and officially decided to kill him, on the ground that he was a dangerous character, a traitor. (John 11:47–53.) Since the seventy members of the Sanhedrin had thus decided, Jesus could no longer go abroad freely. (John 11:54.) The priests and Pharisees sent out an order for anyone who knew the place to which Jesus had fled to apprehend him. (John 11:57.) It was as a result of this general order that Judas Iscariot had Jesus arrested, probably giving information about him promptly, when the placards were put up at the various village corners. For Judas, of course, knew Jesus' whereabouts. This circumstance is set forth clearly in John's Gospel, but not in the Synoptics.

In John 12:27 Jesus is sorrowful because the people

have finally reached the stage where they want to kill him. But having made up his mind that he would come to the Cross, he is ready to face the issue.

Unless we know this atmosphere of Jerusalem, we cannot clearly understand Jesus. The Fourth Gospel, and not the Synoptics, shows us how the plot was developed against Jesus, and especially is this true in the thirteenth, fourteenth and fifteenth chapters.

Through the dramatic portrayal of such circumstances in the Fourth Gospel, we can understand how much Jesus loved the human race, and how he chose the road of his destiny as the Lamb of God. Many critics do not trust the Fourth Gospel, but I do.

JOHN'S DEATH AND THE REVOLUTIONARY PARTY

Jesus was crucified at thirty-three. He began his religio-social movement after John's imprisonment. Up to that time he had worked with John, his teacher. He was not a revolutionist, but he was a patriot. There were anti-taxationists among the revolutionaries who aimed at a boycott on tax-paying. They bitterly opposed the taxes, saying there was no need of paying them, since " no matter how much we pay, it is all carried off to Rome." That party was called the Zealots, or *Zelotes* in Latin. Even among Jesus' disciples there was one called Simon the Zealot. This man was a Leftist of the anti-taxationists. And there were likewise among Jesus' disciples, Rightists, such as Matthew, who believed in collecting taxes and had himself been a tax-collector.

Jesus himself was neither Rightist nor Leftist, but believed in national repentance. Before criticizing our enemies, he urged, let us repent; and whether or not John be killed — that is, without starting a bloody revolution because of John's execution — let us have the Kingdom of God Movement. The Ideal Age appears when man's conscience is born again, and God controls the human race; this is the Kingdom of God. The fundamental thing about the Ideal Age was to be the re-birth of men's consciences. Jesus had to a wonderful degree the power to effect this miracle. Being pure and straight, honest and simple, Jesus laid his finger on and clearly pointed to the moral need of his day. And he did not merely talk about it; he practised it.

There are such folks today among the working people. The laborer who has done the world's work with his own hands, with his own muscles, has a right to speak out clearly. Jesus was that sort. Every word that he spoke was the fruit of his honest, first-hand experience with the hard facts of life.

Yet though he was poor, he came of a good family. Jesus came of the legitimate lineage of King David. And moreover, it is a fact that Jesus himself possessed veritably extraordinary power.

But there was John, in the midst of his active career, killed! This was the way of it. At that time the King still had authority. And John, in the very marketplace of Jerusalem, had dared to criticize the King's adultery. He was therefore accused of the crime of *lèse majesté* and beheaded. It was in the evening of the King's birthday. His head was given, according to her request, to Salome, the daughter of the adulterous woman, as a reward for her dancing at the King's birthday party.

The people would not stand for that. They were stung to the quick. So they planned to start a revolution bearing Jesus upon their shoulders as their king. There were many would-be revolutionists in the time of Jesus. But, lacking military armaments and war funds, they were powerless. When a revolution is hopeless, it is best to start a religious movement. And it is only because Pilate killed Jesus that his name is remembered.

If there are those among us who want to start a revolution, saying, " The present situation is terrible; we can't stand it any longer; let's do something quickly! " it's all right; let them try — but to start a revolution at a time when revolution is hopeless is a foolish performance. The best road to real progress is religion.

How futile is the way of violence is shown by the failure of Amakusa Shiro in the rebellion which he started at Shimabara.* This is a valuable historical example for us to turn to when we are hesitating between the starting of a revolution by violence, or a moral movement. Jesus took more than four hundred years, but finally won out over Rome. If we have patience to endure for four hundred years, we shall find that the superstructure of society will naturally fall to pieces. Social evolution is really like that. Those at the bottom come out on top.

THE CROSS AND THE LAMB

When Jesus first appeared, John said, " This is a great personality. You are the Lamb to bear the sins of the people." (John 1:29.) There is a deep meaning in this. Some men are awake and some are still dreaming. At night we are fast asleep and in the morning we are still dozing. When breakfast-time comes, and we begin to walk dizzily toward the table, we get fully awake for the first time. In a similar way the human race had its semiconscious era which we call the age of the prophets. In

* The Shimabara rebellion, led by Amakusa Shiro, was the effort of the Catholic Christians of three hundred years ago to oppose the government order for their extinction by violence. Amakusa came from the Goto Islands, where even yet Catholic Christianity dating back to that early time is in control, and everyone goes to church on Sunday. But on the mainland all the Shimabara insurrectionists perished.

that half-awake age, pondering the question, "Shall I acknowledge my sin and cry for mercy or shall I not?" part of us is still dozing. At such a time, certain forms of atonement were fashionable. Though a man ought to acknowledge himself in the wrong and ask for pardon, he offers a sheep in his place. Later when they awakened to the point where they said it must be a man who directly offers himself, John pointed to Jesus and declared, "This is the One!"

While man still dozes, he does not understand what he has done when he kills another human being. During the Russo-Japanese war, our soldiers did not think it wrong to kill other men. Having shot their man, they would drop the matter by saying, "That one died, didn't he? It is nothing strange. It is right." We do not think it wrong to kill people in war. When I say war is wrong, people say Kagawa is a dangerous character! And yet it was because war is wrong that we wanted to form the Peace Pact, and even General Tanaka, while Premier, affixed his seal to it.* So different are our insides and outsides that even while we are affixing our national seal to Peace Pacts, anyone inside the nation who speaks against war we dub a traitor. Apparently Japan's official peace movement is aimed at keeping up appearances in the eyes of foreign nations. It is hard to understand our national psychology with reference to world peace. It is not yet clearly thought out.

In the ninth century before Christ the Greeks did not yet think it wrong to commit murder. This we learn from the book, "The Four Seasons of the Grecian Re-

* General Tanaka was the militaristic Premier who brought about the Japanese occupation of Shantung Province in China in 1927, and formulated the policy of imperialism in China now being carried out by the Japanese fascist minority.

ligion." It appears that when the idea of Apollo penetrated the minds of the Greeks they began to think murder
a crime. Similarly in Japan our Kojiki records the development of the idea of evil connected with killing other
human beings.* It is written that when the Japanese
began to realize that it was wrong to kill they wanted to
purify the "six roots of evil," that is, the senses — the
ears, eyes, nose, tongue, body and mind. This purification
was to be accomplished by washing themselves in the river.

Thus when man's inner life begins to develop on the
psychical plane, he awakens from his dreams. At last
reaching the position assumed by Christ, the generality
of human beings came to the point of being willing to
make amends for human blood-shedding.

But Japan is even yet before the dawn. Disarmament
movements in Japan amount to nothing. Premier Hamaguchi wanted disarmament but encountered the opposition
of the war department and his movement perished where
it stood.† It was, moreover, not as enlightened an effort
for disarmament as we need today. It was only the
first faint flush of dawn, and even yet the day is only
beginning in public opinion for disarmament in Japan.

CHRIST AND MOSES' SERPENT

Jesus, however, was thinking of the Whole. When he
heard that someone had committed a fault, he felt that
he himself bore a responsibility for doing the wrong. If
anyone committed suicide because of lack of money, he
felt identified with the unfortunate.

* The Kojiki is the first record of ancient Japanese history beginning
with its mythology.

† Premier Hamaguchi was in office during the recent disarmament
conference at Geneva and favored it. There was an attempt upon his
life by a reactionary which resulted in his death about nine months later.
The tide turned in the opposite direction.

This sort of consciousness was strong in him. That was his starting point from the very beginning. He wanted to make amends to God for human sin; to start a movement to re-make the human conscience; to clean up this soiled world. He was resolved to be lifted up, as Moses lifted up the serpent in the wilderness. At the time of their emancipation from slavery the Hebrews had disobeyed God's command and made miscegenetic marriages with Moabitish women. God told them to stop that, but many thousands went ahead and married the Moabites and serpents were sent among them as punishment. There was the tradition that at that time there was one way only by which they could be saved — to repent and look up to a serpent lifted up on a pole. It was immediately after John was put in prison that Jesus got the idea that he also was to be lifted up like that serpent.

The Righteous One must suffer. Loving others and selfishness, do not go together. Money-lending and the labor movement just don't fit into one personality. From a selfish point of view, the radical is bad; while from the point of view of the radical, the narrow nationalist is not good for the country. Thus selfishness and love are always in disagreement. To take the loving course of action is the right thing, of course, but yet we think it wrong to do so.

When John the Baptist denounced the King's immorality, he was executed. Then Jesus concluded that if John had been killed, he also would surely be done away with; for he thought, " John understood and taught only a part of the gospel, while I teach it a hundred percent! " Calling good, good, and evil, evil, Jesus thought it was a foregone conclusion that he would be executed.

From the time of John's execution, Jesus announced

explicitly that he was to be executed. This is clearly set forth in the Fourth Gospel. Jesus said that his body was to be broken as the Bread of Life for the multitude. (John 6:35.) He himself could not commit murder. He could not lead the five thousand or the four thousand in a revolution. However, the disciples did not understand. They were always thinking: "Jesus is a great man. Presently he will become king, and we shall be his cabinet ministers." But then Jesus brought forth this disastrous idea that within a short time he would be arrested and executed! In John 6:15 the crowd, exasperated at the execution of the Baptist, wanted to take Jesus and force him to be king. But in John 15:13 Jesus clearly showed that he was facing toward his own impending death: " Greater love hath no man than this, that a man should lay down his life for his friends." And a little earlier he was talking about a grain of wheat! (John 12:24.) In human evolution someone must be pinned under, someone must become the foundation. Thus before his crucifixion Jesus gave the farewell cup to his disciples and taught them. The Fourth Gospel shows this clearly.

Also on the other hand, the situation in the government is recorded. According to the Fourth Gospel, Jesus himself was partly responsible for the circumstances which led to his execution. From the moment that he had launched out on his religious revolution, it might have been anticipated. The government thought that if it did not execute Jesus, the country would come to destruction; Jesus himself thought that if he did not die, he would be too ashamed of himself to go on: and since it was written in the scriptures that unless someone died the world's sin would not be redeemed — these three reasons were cumulative. Jesus thinking that he must bear the sin of mankind, the government also thinking it best to do away with him, and the scriptures saying there is no salvation without the death of someone — since these three causes reinforced each other, Jesus hung on the Cross.

THE GRAIN OF WHEAT TEACHING

But the multitude do not understand it! They continue to think it a very peculiar thing that Jesus should die. Neither do the disciples understand it! "That such a teacher should die is unthinkable!" The government, however, continues to think the death of such a low fellow a desirable thing.

Whatever the government or the people think of it, there emerges a new meaning in the Fourth Gospel for this event. It says that this shedding of innocent blood means that the human race must awaken from its dreaming and become deeply, yea, bloodily, in earnest in confessing and repenting of its sins. This death has been according to the scriptures, this Gospel says, and it will be understood when interpreted by the Holy Spirit. We disciples did not understand Jesus when he was alive, but we understand him since his death. As long as we look with the eyes of the flesh, we do not understand it. (John 14:26.) Many people think that it is all right to commit a little evil for the sake of achieving a great good. But we prefer to meditate on Jesus' patience and the Cross. As the soul gradually comes to full consciousness, the wickedness of murder, or of the use of any violence, dawns upon it, and at the same time it grasps the meaning of the great love of Jesus.

This sacrificial love, giving up one's own life, surrendering everything to God, is like the business of seed-sowing. The seed has to be buried first, but soon the spring time arrives, and it comes out again. So long as the human race is suffering, someone must become a sacrifice. Unless we grasp this great truth and expect to be sown like the seed, we cannot bring about the progress of civilization.

During a visit to the Kangyo Bank, I was told that students sent through school by the sacrifices of older sisters or other relatives make very much better records than boys whose background is one of luxury. The former can, and the latter cannot, be trusted with tens of thousands of yen or any amount of money. There is the element of sacrifice in the background of those who can be trusted. Those who know themselves to be worthless, but who feel gratitude and appreciation for the sacrifice that Jesus has made for them, are to be trusted.

Since the heart of God mingles with the heart of Jesus, and the heart of Jesus with the heart of God, I, too, must live a life of sacrifice, in the spirit of Jesus who died for the sins of the human race. So long as I am unawakened, the Cross of Jesus seems never to have had any existence. Nevertheless for nineteen hundred years Jesus has captured the hearts of men, because he set his seal to the fact that his death was a death of redemption. There are many biographies of Karl Marx, but the biography of Jesus Christ is the one that grips men more. That is because, the more we meditate upon it, the more the race begins to understand this fully conscious, fully awakened spirit of Jesus. Through imbibing this spirit of Jesus, and lifting up our souls to the level of the Cross, we become able to kneel in the Presence of God. At this point, the evolution of the universe becomes inner and spiritual.*

* This statement should be connected with the line in the introductory poem on page 6.

PRAYER

Father God: Though we in our unworthy footsteps are carelessly and constantly creating sin, and the sins of others are even more careless, we are grateful that Jesus made amends for us by hanging on the Cross. Forgive our sins, both conscious and unconscious, and wash and cleanse us through the Blood of Christ. Cause the spirit of Christ to fill and permeate us, we beseech Thee. Send light into our clouded souls, that we may be enabled to lay hold of our responsibility for the sins of Capitalism, and take upon ourselves the burden of redeeming the sins of capitalistic greed, bolshevistic destructiveness, and eroticism.

Filled with the spirit of Christ, enable us to think seriously of the sins of the world. May the grace of Christ, who shed his blood, utterly fill us. We pray through Christ. Amen.

> " In the history of the human race there is needed
> The creation of this Cross-consciousness
> That is to say, the creation of
> The inner life of its very soul."

The " evolution of the universe becoming inner and spiritual " means much the same thing as " the creation of the inner life of the very soul " of the human race.

V

THE CROSS IN THE THOUGHT OF PAUL

For Christ did not send me to baptize but to preach the good news — but not with fine language, or the cross of Christ might seem an empty thing. For to those who are on their way to destruction, the story of the cross is nonsense, but to us who are to be saved, it means all the power of God. For the scripture says, " I will destroy the wisdom of the wise, And I will thwart the shrewdness of the shrewd." I Corinthians 1:17–19. (Goodspeed.)

As IT IS stated in these words by the Apostle Paul, the word of the Cross is foolishness to those who are perishing. Moreover, the Jews demand signs and the Greeks seek wisdom. The crucified Christ whom Paul was preaching seemed to them a mere impertinence. (I Cor. 2:22–23.) Paul could be patient with them, for he himself had formerly misunderstood the whole meaning of the life of Christ. To begin with, he had despised him, thinking him merely an ordinary person, and so had persecuted the religion which sprang up around him. But as soon as Paul understood his error, he repented decisively, and adhered to the religion of the Cross.

Of Paul's thirteen epistles, the earlier ones do not contain any systematic exposition of the Cross. Just before writing them, during his first missionary journey, he underwent many trials. You might expect, therefore, that he would have written more about the Cross in those first epistles, but it is a fact that in I and II Thessalonians there is not as much as we might wish. It is when we reach Galatians that we begin to find Paul writing of the Cross with passionate power: " Our Lord Jesus Christ, who to save us from this present wicked world, gave himself for our sins, at the will of our God and Father — to him be glory forever. Amen." (Gal. 1:4–5.)

Galatians is one of Paul's earlier letters, and in its first chapter we find him giving his witness, it may be with the intention of telling his own life-story up to the time of his discovery of the Cross of Christ. Verses 4 and 5 give Paul's clear conception of Christ. Up to the time of his conversion, not knowing the purpose of Christ's coming, Paul had persecuted him, or rather his followers. But now Christ had condescended to live within Paul himself. And there had been brought to birth within him such a faith as that he now could say that he would gladly die for the sake of Christ. Thus, this Cross is good news of real forgiveness even for such a one as himself — a man with a criminal record behind him! He had entered into the assured confidence that he had been forgiven. (Gal. 2:16–21.)

Paul admits that he has really no right to be alive at all. He had put to death the folks who were blabbing around about the Christ-superstition! It was, to be sure, in ignorance. At the time he had thought it right. He himself had not thought it necessary for Christ to die! . . . What an impudent thing! . . . for a common carpenter to presume to die for the sins of others! . . . that is the way his mind had run on, formerly. But when he drew near to the character of Christ, the carpenter, Paul more and more became confident that through the death of that common laborer Christ his own sins had been forgiven.

That was Paul's fresh point of departure. Hitherto he had been looking at Christ from a purely external, superficial standpoint; therefore he had completely misunderstood and opposed him. "That worthless common fellow, that toiler, that proletarian Jesus, a boor who has no standing in the world of men whatever; that Jesus, the son of a poor low-down father, a carpenter, without any education, of a much lower intellectual scale than mine —probably he didn't even know his scriptures!" That is the way Paul thought, and looked down on him with contempt, as today we despise the beggars by the roadside. Paul himself had come of a good family, a wealthy one; he had graduated from the university, and moreover as an honor student! (Gal. 1:14.)

Nevertheless, the more he thought about the character of Christ, the more he realized that the Christ whom formerly he had thought contemptible, had not after all died wantonly or accidentally, but as a sacrifice for him, for Paul himself, to bring him, Paul, into intimate relations with God, to attach him to God forever. Paul's whole life was changed, and he found himself in intimate personal relations with Christ. And the reason why we want to become conscious of the truth about the Cross of Christ is this same reason, that is, that we may gain personal relations with Christ.

THE CROSS OF EXPERIENCE

It is easy for the average person to grasp the concept of God, but not that of the Cross. Many will say, "Our days are different from those of Christ who died nineteen hundred years ago. Besides, though he was rather great, he was after all nothing but a mere man like ourselves, and a carpenter at that —a Jew— at all events a human being no different from ourselves. What do you mean by saying that he went through all sorts of suffering for all mankind?" This they say because they do not see his inner experience of love. But if in the course of our spiritual development we can once get beyond all this external appearance, and dwell on how much Christ was able to love man no matter how deep in sin, and moreover, if we can focus our thoughts on how we ourselves can be related to this love of Christ — then that love of Christ is reborn in our breasts.

That is what Paul is saying in the closing part of the second chapter of Galatians: "For it is through the law that I have become dead to the law, so that I may live for God." (Gal. 2:19.) The law is the moral code. From the point of view of God's moral code, there is not one perfect human being. But Christ's dying for us means that " I have been crucified with Christ, and it is no longer I that live; Christ lives within me." Paul is continually repeating this. His view of the Cross, and Christ's view of the Cross, are different. Christ's cross is dying for mankind, absolutely for the other person, while Paul is the recipient, the person who is died for. Christ's Cross is the absolute. Paul's Cross is a Cross of receiving. Since Christ purposes to die for men, his cross is a brave, courageous one; Paul's is that of One who died for me. In that, Christ's Christianity and Paul's Christianity are different, and the critics know it.

The first thing that Paul wrote was that he himself had been crucified with Christ, and that the life he was now living was through the grace of Christ who had died for him. As Christ emptied himself, I also am to cast away this sinful self. And when self has been extinguished, for the first time I return to real living. Paul thinks of the Cross-experience as like the shedding of its old chrysalis on the part of the butterfly. The larva has to pass through

that stage before it can become a butterfly. And in the
human realm, unless man passes through that experience
of the Cross, he does not become a genuine human being.
Things are simply not right unless, on the Cross, I shed
my old, empty, outworn shell, and leave it behind. The
Cross means to be able, once for all, to cast away the
" flesh," to be enabled to nail to the Cross this unworthy,
limited, and putrefying physical nature of mine. Christ
did that for me, Paul says.

I want to think further of this.

Christ himself does not think of the Cross in this light.
He does not have the thought of shedding his skin on the
Cross, but only of fulfilling scripture. But when we get
to Paul, the Cross-thought becomes the philosophy of the
serpent! Since Christ died once, Paul has it that we
also have died, have been executed with Christ on the
Cross. We are in danger of interpreting this in a mere
" spiritual " sense, to say that Christ's dying was a spiritual thing, not a matter of the flesh. But Paul takes it
as a reality. " *This* flesh was hung on the Cross." Christ's
being nailed on the Cross was the same as his own dying,
and so he writes as if he himself had been crucified. This
experience has not yet filled our breasts, as it had Paul's.
Paul had been engaged in the dastardly business of killing
Christians. That was why he had a deeper, more real, experience than ours. Christ's dying was for us. It was
the same as if Christ had died instead of Paul himself being
executed as a murderer. He has no right to be alive at
all, he says.

In order to attain to this spirit of Paul, we must meditate yet more. Our intuition is not yet like that of Paul.
Iron will not melt when heated merely with a fire of
straw or kindling. It melts only at a temperature of 1600°
to 2000°. It is because the fire of our love for Christ is

not yet hot enough that we do not understand. Paul
said, "It is no longer I that live but Christ lives within
me." This also we do not feel as Paul did. We do not feel
the *grace* of Christ as Paul did. Living along in our dull
way, unconsciously or only semi-consciously, we do not
sense that "my being alive is by the grace of Christ."

The ancient Samurai had this thought. In classic
Japanese drama there are many examples of people who
lived because someone else had died for their sakes. Modern folks, however, have very little realization of the
fact that "my being alive at all is because there has been
someone else who has died as a substitute for me." To
Paul, Christ's death was a death of vicarious substitution,
of redemption. Deep in his own heart he knew that Christ
had died for him. That substitution was not merely
"spiritual." Christ had really taken his place. He was
a criminal, with no right to be alive at all. This thought
continues on through Galatians.

SALVATION THROUGH ONE MAN

In the next epistle, I Corinthians, the Cross is the main
subject of the first two chapters. After these there is
not much about it. It is the same with II Corinthians.
In this II Corinthians there is still less concerning it than
in I Corinthians. But when we come to Romans, it is
almost entirely the meaning of the Cross that Paul was
thinking of, as in Galatians. And this meaning is more
fully developed because Paul is now writing after long
meditation. Although elsewhere I call Romans the Gospel of Grace, yet, from a different aspect, it may also
be called the philosophical exposition of the Cross. In
Romans Paul takes up and discusses all the different aspects of the philosophical problems connected with the
Cross.

One of these problems is this: although Christ died as a redeemer, the days and months have passed by, and one wonders whether this one sacrifice of the Christ who died as an individual will avail for the many. That is, appraising Christ's heroic death numerically or quantitatively, it just does not seem to fit the situation. No matter how great Christ may have been, it does seem queer to think that he died for the entire human race. Isn't it impossible for one individual to die for many? Thus, it seems, the adequacy of Christ's redemption had become a matter for problematical discussion among the brethren. As they reached the point of saying, " Oh, no! really, such a thing would be impossible," Paul argued for it in the epistle to the Romans. (Romans 5:12-21.)

Paul answers this question by an inverse process of reasoning. He explains Christ through the system that put evil in circulation in the world. If, he says, through one man sin came, if one man's sin can affect all, in the same way if one man redeems, all are redeemed. This, he says, is logical in view of the social solidarity of the human race. As from one man sin was passed on to society, so, if one assumes responsibility for making love regnant in society, this love will reach all the people and be revealed for the redemption of the whole human race.*

Paul saw this Cross-redemption idea not only quantitatively, however, but also as a deep redemption of the whole nature, temperament, and disposition. This is the

---

* *Responsibility* in Kagawa's usage and to the Japanese in general is a very broad term, hard to fully interpret into English, but connected with the concept of social solidarity referred to in a previous footnote. Paul had this social consciousness of the " whole family in heaven and on earth," centering up in God, and of his individual responsibility toward it. Instead of changing the word here, may we suggest to the reader to make a note of it, and secure an interpretation of it through Kagawa's use of the term in later chapters?

thought in Romans six, seven and eight. In chapter six there is the same idea as in Galatians (Romans 6:1–6). Here Paul is not speaking of skin-shedding; he is thinking of it as grafting. We have the Cross lineage. We have both bad and good in our heredity. We can be brought to the Cross of Christ and grafted upon it: "For if we have been planted together in the likeness of his death, we shall be also in the likeness of his resurrection." (Romans 6:5.) We, like Christ, must die once. Christ was executed and we too must bear responsibility. And, moreover, we too must die for the sins of the whole of humanity. Christ's death was not a mere death. He had to undergo punishment for the crimes of the human race. Since Christ underwent that punishment, if I also undergo that punishment, I come back to life with a feeling like that of the Resurrection.

Paul saw the Cross as punishment. Christ endured punishment, as one who had been guilty of insubordination to the Roman empire. Though Christ himself had committed no sin, yet he suffered punishment, moreover, from the God of heaven and earth. And so he died for the whole human race. God loves the human race with a profound love. If he should punish evildoers, as evil, the race would become extinct. Therefore he punished Christ alone, and thereafter any who drew near to Christ would be forgiven by God. This was Paul's interpretation of the Cross as punishment. It does not appeal to us. We like to think only of God's love and not of the justice of our receiving punishment from God. That is because we cannot acquire Paul's painful, anguished feeling of responsibility, of deserving punishment from God.

Paul, since he himself had committed murder, thought he ought to be crucified, and that if he were not to be crucified, it was because Christ had become a vicarious sacrifice for him and forgiven him. He considered himself the chief of sinners, and that Christ had died for this chief of sinners, and therefore though he had the gift of life now, that life was not for him to use for himself. This idea is summed up in the 24th and 25th verses of the seventh chapter of Romans: "O wretched man that I am! Who shall deliver me from the body of this death? I thank God through Jesus Christ our Lord. So then with the mind I myself serve the law of God; but with the flesh the law of sin."

THE CRYSTALLIZATION OF HOLY LOVE

When we come to the eighth chapter of Romans, its conception of Christ is not merely the human Christ, but Christ as the crystallization of the love of God. It is Christ who crystallized, as love, the Spirit which fills the universe. Whoever is constrained by the love of Christ will transcend his age and natural status, socially, politically, morally. This is stated in Romans 8:35 ff.

From the ninth chapter on, Paul takes an historical view which shows that the revelation of the love of Christ has not been merely sudden or sporadic. God's love has been gradually, and more and more deeply, revealed, until like the swelling of a great crescendo in a vast symphony it reached its climax in Christ.

After that, in prison, Paul wrote Philemon, but in this epistle the Cross is not directly mentioned. Paul is conscious, however, of the process of redemption. To Philemon he writes, " Brother, you were a slave of sin and have been emancipated. Therefore it is your duty to emancipate your human slave."

In Colossians he writes of the Cross as the profound purpose of God. " In whom we have redemption through his blood, even the forgiveness of sins." (Col. 1:14.)

" And having made peace through the blood of his Cross, by him to reconcile all things unto himself; by him, I say, whether they be things in earth or things in heaven." (Col. 1:21.)

Here also there is little difference from the theme of Galatians. There is the body of Christ confronting the punishment of God; it is through the fact that Christ bore our punishment for us that we have been forgiven. That was God's plan, he says. This same sort of thing appears in Col. 2:3–15: " And having spoiled principalities and powers, he made a show of them openly, triumphing over them in it." (Col. 2:15.) Thus he writes of the "triumph" of the Cross. For naturally in God's sight we are all deserving of execution, we all deserve to be put to death — and the fact that we are alive today is solely because the Christ of the Cross is putting forth tremendous efforts for us.

Paul's view of the Cross is passive; it is a process of being acted upon. " And we are complete in him, which is the head of all principality and power: In whom also ye are circumcised with the circumcision made without hands, in putting off the body of the sins of the flesh by the circumcision of Christ." (Col. 2:10–11.) (This "circumcision" of Christ means the Cross. It is a mystical skin-shedding of the spirit.)

Ephesians has in the main the same point of view as Colossians, but expresses it in a deeply mystical fashion: " In whom we have our redemption through his blood, the forgiveness of our trespasses, according to the riches of his grace." (Eph. 1:7.) That this redemption is the forgiveness of sins, is many times repeated. In Ephesians 2:14 it is written that through the Cross, God and man are unified. And at the beginning of the fifth chapter is written: " Walk in love, even as Christ also loved you, and gave Himself up for us, an offering and a sacrifice to God for an odor of a sweet smell." (Eph. 5:2.)

When we reach Philippians Paul's thought becomes even more mystical, and we know that he is mastered by a wonderful emotion. "It is no longer I that live," he says. "I am caused to live by Christ." It is recorded that he is caused to live transcendently. Paul is able to live a life which has crossed the death line because Christ has emptied himself and died on the Cross. (Phil. 2:6–9.) Therefore Paul is not talking merely about the Cross that brought Christ's life to an end at thirty-three. He is thinking about an extension of the Cross, a Cross which existed from before the time of Christ's birth, which continued and was prolonged and was revealed at the last at thirty-three — a Cross which magnified Christ's whole life — the Cross in Christ's own definition of it is as a universal Cross.*

After that Paul wrote three more letters, in which the message about the Cross does not differ much from that of Philippians.

THE TWO ASPECTS OF THE CROSS

Christ went forward actively to the act of taking the Cross upon himself. Paul, on the other hand, takes it that he, Paul, is being acted upon by the Cross. Christ died as a gift that he was giving to us; Paul's interpretation of the Cross is that Christ died for our sins. This came from his strong impression of his own crimes and sins. So Christ's Cross is a very brave and courageous one, while Paul's is a bloody and anguished one.

Then is there a contradiction between Paul's Cross and

* The idea these words "extension," "continued," "prolonged," are intended to convey is that of the universal cross mentioned at the close of the paragraph, the cross in which we all participate, the cross of Galatians 2:20. This is really the main subject of the book.

that of Christ? No! There is no contradiction whatever between Christ's Cross and the Cross of Paul's hu-
miliation. The more Paul tasted it personally, the more
he understood that he himself must bear the Cross. His
life was not his own. It was Christ's. This is the conclusion to which he was forced. We too must realize that
Christ has forgiven us and taken punishment for us.

It was entirely because he held the point of view of God
that Christ aimed to give the Cross to the human race.
Starting from God, the Cross is the crystallization of
love. The fact, unique in the whole world, of Christ's
sacrificing himself and shedding the blood of redemption
for the sins of the race, is the very revelation of Love
itself.

Seen from our narrow human viewpoint, this is by no
means a matter of being spoiled by God's love. To man,
fouled by sin, Christ's death contains punishment as well
as love. Man is separated from God. His selfish instincts
easily separate him from God. To kill these on the Cross
involves a kind of selection, the elimination of the lower instincts by a selective process in favor of higher impulses
which, from the point of view of selfish man, can be thought
of as a kind of punishment. But unless these selfish instincts are killed, he cannot reach up toward God. Only
after he has fully endured punishment can the perfect
image of man-united-with-God make its appearance in
him. Thus Paul believes that through Christ's having
submitted himself to endure God's punishment for the
whole human race, that which is merely human in us human beings dies, and the Godlike human being emerges.

Paul thought that for a man to be executed because of
his own crime was characteristic of the old pattern of the
sons of Adam. But for a pure personality, unstained by
crime, to attain to such a consciousness of sacrificial social

solidarity as to die gladly a death of redemption for others, taking upon himself the full responsibility for the sins of the whole human race — for him to rise to such a level meant that even while enduring punishment for men, he as a man had well-nigh entered the same condition as that of God.

To Paul this was the perfect working of conscience in the perfect man — for him, being a perfect person, to make confession of and reparation for the crimes of the whole human race before God. At that, Paul, fixing his eyes on Christ, was conscious that through believing in him, his own crimes were entirely forgiven, and that through the rebound of Christ's Spirit into his own heart, the life of love, not of the first but of the second Adam, was resurrected in him. As in the human body the blood circulates and repairs old wounds and even makes the wounded place new and perfect again, so Christ, making amends for old damages, performs the functions of blood circulation for the human race in the new man created by his sacrificial death on the Cross.

Paul's becoming conscious of this metabolism-through-love was a source of joy and thankfulness to him. We moderns completely fail to understand this redemptive burden-bearing. Modern folks understand only love, and do not fathom the fact that Christ put forth his energy and struggled to make up for man's shortcomings in order to restore him to his destined perfection.

This Christ who had thus perfectly made compensation had also, Paul believed, been caused to stand before God as the perfect pattern of the race and its representative man. And Paul was profoundly convinced that as the first Adam had been created by God, this Second Adam, that is, Christ, was the revelation from God — God's superlative means of disclosing his love to men.

Inspired by this grace, Paul believed that even though the Christ of history had left this world, yet, through him — that is, through the power of the Holy Spirit — the love of God flows in the spirit of man and possesses it.

PARTICIPATION IN THE CROSS

His crimes forgiven, Paul believed that through living in close association with Christ he had been granted the privilege also of participation in Christ's Cross of suffering. " Now I rejoice in my sufferings for your sake, and fill up on my part what is lacking in the afflictions of Christ in my flesh for his body's sake, which is the church;" he says in Col. 1:24. This word, church, is really *ecclesia* in the original. When translated, as in the Japanese, as " kyo-kai," literally, " teaching-society," it seems like an extremely narrow and limited club intended for cultural purposes only. I am convinced that it ought to be translated as " holy society." To Paul, Christ's death was for the purpose of creating a holy society and moreover this continuous and progressive creation of the holy society would forever be needing the Cross type of love. The Christ who came revealed in human form had left the world; had left it for the sake of revealing that Cross-Love. But Paul felt that he himself, who had also in a small way travailed in the birth of the Cross-love, had become a participator in it, a second Christ, and that he must needs participate in this movement of Love-through-suffering.

Almost the same thought can be discovered in the epistle to the Philippians to which he addressed his pen some time after writing to the Colossians. In Phil. 1:29, he says, " Because to you it hath been granted in the behalf of Christ, not only to believe on him, but also to suffer in his behalf." Here Paul is meditating on suffering as a blessing. Paul thought the inheritance of the Cross to be a blessing. Brought to new life through it, Paul was aware that he himself must bear the Cross in his turn for others. He who has been redeemed by blood must carry on this work of the Cross. The Christ-love must forever go on rescuing humanity from its crimes and misery, must not stint its sacrifices until the last human tear has been wiped away. Paul was completely mastered by the spirit of Christ.

Thus Christ's Gospel and Paul's Gospel do not contradict each other, as some German theologians erroneously suppose. It is through Paul that Christ's love first comes fully to consciousness; this I have discovered. Of course, as I said before, it will never do to forget that while Christ was animated by active redeeming love to the uttermost, Paul passively gave thanks for and accepted this redeeming love as grace revealed through Christ, and with confession and gratitude gave thanks to God and Christ that his sins had been forgiven.

Only those who are conscious of the Whole realize their responsibility for the Whole. Unless one enters into consciousness of the Whole, a consciousness like that of God, one would not have redemptive consciousness which depends upon a sense of responsibility for the past. Such an era of rampant individualism as the eighteenth and nineteenth centuries would naturally be the last to comprehend Christ's redeeming love as Paul did. The more Paul felt shame for his former treason against God, the more he felt the value of Christ's blood which had flowed on the Cross.

PRAYER

Father God: We are filled with deep joy to know that Christ died for us, though we do not comprehend that solemn historical fact, and, no matter how much we think about it, we cannot exhaust the meaning of that deep Providence — that from the one man, Christ, came redemption for the whole human race, and power for cleansing from the nailing to the Cross of this One. Even when we fail, cause us to reverence and look up to Christ and lead us one by one to cleansing in the blood of the Cross. We pray through Christ. Amen.

VI

THE CROSS AS REVEALED IN PAUL'S PARABLES

For if, while we were enemies, we were reconciled to God through the death of his Son, much more, being reconciled, shall we be saved by his life. Romans 5:10.

WE DO NOT realize that the Cross is the center of Christianity. We are likely to go only so far as to think that Christ's sacrifice makes a deep impression upon men, and is therefore precious, and that Christ is an ideal personality. The bloody agony which renounced life itself does not come home to our hearts. This is because our way of thinking of sin is not as deep as Christ's. If we are living a fairly good life, we are satisfied and have no thought of assuming responsibility for the sins of others. We are too content with living from day to day.

But merely not to do evil is to be no different from the stones in the roadway. Better to be a block of wood than to be self-complacent at taking care of self alone! If we are merely avoiding sin, we do not need redemption. But when once we get to feeling, as God does, a responsibility for the sins of the whole human race, we cannot remain in idleness. Idleness and indifference in the face of this sinful world are in themselves sins. It is a sin to seek escape from the turmoil of the world by flight to the mountains. Among the parables of Christ there is the one about the talents. The men-servants who had been entrusted with the five and with the two talents set the money to work and gained double, but the one talent man simply put away what had been entrusted to him. When their master returned, he reproved this servant for not setting his money to work, and said, " If that was all you were going to do with it, why did you not at the very least put my money into a bank? " And then, " Give your talent to the five-talent man." Thus Christ taught that merely to do nothing is unpardonable.

My conscience pricks me when I am doing nothing, even when forced to rest by illness. I think to myself in shame that while there are many sick people who do a great work by writing letters, I am merely concerned with curing my own sickness! When you are contented with a small life and a small measure of success, when you are content with selfish, individualistic gratification you do not really need redemption. When we are content with such a selfish life, we cannot possibly understand how much Christ suffered for the salvation of the race.

Christ thought of sin as God does. Paul also examined himself, with a profound consciousness of his sin, and said: " Faithful is the saying, and worthy of all acceptation, that Christ Jesus came into the world to save sinners; of whom I am chief." I am the captain of all criminals, he is saying remorsefully. But had he committed some great crime? He had not committed adultery. He had not stolen. He had not killed anyone with his own hands. Nevertheless he examined himself, and because he had been enlightened by God, he had a deep consciousness of sin.

Paul was rather better than the average Jew. But compared to God, compared to Christ, he had lived below the right standard. Moreover, even considering his education and ancestry, he knew he ought to have done better. So he thought of himself as the chief of sinners; for when Christ had done so much for the human race, he, Paul, had misinterpreted it, and had rejoiced in the killing of Christ's disciples. He was terribly ashamed of this. To be sure he had been ignorant, and so might reasonably have been forgiven. But when he examined himself, when he laid bare his faults, he realized that he must repent before God.

People today have a very dull sense of sin. When they are brought to account for their own failures, they blame their circumstances in life, the economic system, or something else, and do not admit any responsibility themselves. Their ideas of the Atonement are hazy. But anyone who, like Paul, has thought seriously about his sins, cannot get along without someone like Christ to lovingly forgive them.

PAUL'S VIEW OF REDEMPTION

Paul thinks seven things about sin. Carelessly glanced at these may seem hard to understand, but even a little application of thought to them brings out the clear meaning of Christ's Atonement.*

1. First of all, Paul thought that sin is opposed to life.

* " In a brief but delightful conversation with Kagawa, I asked him what he really thought about the atonement; did he hold the substitutionary theory? With his characteristic eagerness and facility, he replied, ' I think just as Paul did. Paul felt that there was something wrong with man, and Christ could set him right. When Paul tried to say what was wrong with man, he used seven parables. Now it was a debtor whose debts must be paid; again a condemned criminal to be reprieved; or a burdened traveler to be relieved; a sick man to be healed; a dead man to be raised; a slave to be emancipated, or a wandering child to be brought home. But ' he said, with his face aglow, ' Paul didn't care which parable you used, or if you used some other. All he cared about was that man was somehow wrong and Christ could set him right.' " (William Pierson Merrill, in Scribner's Magazine, reprinted in The Christian, December 23, 1933.)

" What fruit then had ye at that time in the things whereof ye are now ashamed? for the end of those things is death. But now being made free from sin and become servants to God, ye have your fruit unto sanctification, and the end eternal life. For the wages of sin is death; but the free gift of God is eternal life in Christ Jesus our Lord." (Romans 6:21–23.) In teaching this, Paul taught that the result of sin is death. He thought that sin is the very opposite of life. People today think that a moderate amount of sinning will not affect their lives, that sin and life are two different matters. But the result of such sinning leads to death! The individual, or the society, that indulges in sin, is on its way to death. A nation which kills other people, and thus sows hatred and enmity, will come to destruction as a result of its national wild oats.

2. Next, sin is a schism, a conflict, it is disintegration. This is taught in the middle of the second chapter of the Ephesian epistle. If my spirit is disintegrated, divided, it is therefore distracted, and deranged. And if society is schismatic, and divided, it is thereby destroyed. Sin causes the disunion of individual personality and the break-up of society. Through sin, any harmony between instincts and consciousness becomes unobtainable. Thinking of this, Paul cried, in Romans 7:24: " Wretched man that I am! Who shall deliver me from the body of this death? "

3. Again, he thinks of sin as loss, in the sense of failure in business. In the eighth chapter of Romans he says that he is ashamed because we are living an insufficient life, full of contradictions. That is, sin is atrophy, a phenomenon of degeneracy, leading to ruin, wreck, collapse, downfall.

4. Next, sin is straying away from the pathway. Separated from God's purpose, unable to do the good he

wants to do, having perforce to do the evil he does not want to do, man is in agony.

5. Again, sin is being outside the law. Having been given the aim of becoming a child of God, he becomes instead a son of anger, a son of cursing — that is sin! This is taught in the fifth and sixth chapters of Romans.

Thus sin is opposed to life. Paul realized poignantly that he was a divided personality, outside the law, that he was missing the mark.

THE PARABLE OF BLOOD

The Cross is therefore explained in suitable parables as power to redeem from sin. Paul thought of blood as that which revives life from sin, which opposes life. Blood is the source of physical life. " For scarcely for a righteous man will one die: for peradventure for a good man some one would even dare to die." (Romans 5:7.) "Wherefore whosoever shall eat the bread or drink the cup of the Lord in an unworthy manner, shall be guilty of the body and the blood of the Lord." (I Corinthians 11:27.) Besides these verses, in many other places in Paul's writings, Christ's blood is the phrase most commonly used.

But to get God to save from past sin means not merely getting physical blood to work. Mere physical blood cannot save from sin, which is spiritual. It is not because blood flows that past sins are redeemed. What this means is that Christ has given the power of life through love, of life which is conveyed by the blood. The blood, with its power of metabolism repairs the damages in the body. It restores the broken form and can even bring new life into that which is no longer able to work. Love is also like that. If you love people you can bring new life into the broken form.

Christ's loving men was not merely with the lips. He

loved them to the extent of shedding his blood. This shedding of this blood was the culmination of his love. So although blood was used primarily as a parable, it gets to be that the blood itself saves. John explains blood as having a mystical power. Blood cleanses away the filth of the body. Gathering it all together, it carries it to the heart, and then on to the lungs, and there purifies it with oxygen. Thus " the blood of Jesus his Son cleanseth us from all sin." The love of Christ itself engulfs all the filth and washes it away! What precious blood this is! Paul gave thanks, because he had experienced that through it we are saved from all our sins.

THE PARABLE OF THE ARMY

Next, Paul sees the Cross as the means of breaking down the stone walls of ill will between people. He shows two opposing forces which had come into conflict brought into one. " For he is our peace, who hath made both one, and brake down the middle wall of partition, having abolished in his flesh the enmity, even the law of commandments contained in ordinances; that he might create of the two one new man, so making peace; and might reconcile them both in one body unto God through the Cross, having slain the enmity thereby." (Eph. 2:14–16.)

Maeterlinck once said, there are two " horns " in the world, which have been fighting each other since the dawn of history and will be embroiling the peoples of Europe in killing each other to the end of time. These are the Teutons and the Gauls. A certain Japanese Lutheran pastor, who studied in Germany during the world war, lamented that during that whole time he did not once hear a sermon on the text, " Love your enemies." Ill will is indeed a fearful thing. Resentment causes people to oppose each other with terrible antagonism. Greece and

Rome fought each other and both were destroyed. If you or your nation fight too much you too will be annihilated.

On the other hand, in South America, Argentina and Chile, though they fought for a long time, at length made peace, and a covenant to help one another, and placed a great figure of Christ on the boundary between them, on top of the Andes mountains. One arm is lifted in blessing Argentina and one is blessing Chile. Thus Christ counteracts the antagonism between two opposing powers. It would be like the Genji and Heike * clasping hands to work together for Japan.

In Christ's parable, Beelzebub's fighting against himself is a bad business — he will fall. Sin is fighting against God, it is division of the personality. God and man can be reconciled through Christ. Whether the home or the nation, both are unified through the emergence of love. When man and God were fighting one another, through the appearance of Christ they were reconciled. Through the love of Christ, God's love was revealed as wanting to save man, and man got into the mood of wanting to return to God. Through the Cross of Christ the two, hitherto divided, were united, as Paul explains.

THE PARABLE OF LOSS

Third, Paul says that redemption is the work of making up for *loss*. He illustrates it by the blood-circulation with its action of metabolism. There are those who say that because God is love, he could not allow punishment. But that is too easy. It is like saying that because God is love, that when you put water into a bag with a hole in it, that the hole in the bag won't matter! You must close up the

* The Genji and Heike were opposing clans who fought to the death for supremacy in what has been called the " Japanese Wars of the Roses."

hole! Unless you fill up the hole, the bag won't hold water, and your heart cannot receive the love of God. You can't reveal the glory of God, if you have a hole in your bag, no matter how much of God's glory you receive. It is Christ who fills up that egregious hole.

The blood circulation has the power to heal wounds. My child once got a bad bruise on his nose at a friend's house. I was anxious as to whether it would ever heal up, but while I was worrying about it, the blood cured it and made the nose-form as it had been before. I thought it marvelous. Crabs are like that. If one of the claws of a crab is torn off, the next year a new claw is sure to grow. A pig's hindparts if cut off will grow again fat and round.

Love creates the same pattern anew. It redeems the place that was lost. To the measure of its depth, the love of God can perfectly heal the holes of the past, and all its sins. It does not merely repair the damages of sin, but even transforms that which has been broken into perfect health, perfect working capacity. Peter's life illustrates that. Many times he failed and tore holes in his bag of life. Through Christ his holes were filled up, and he even attained to starting a great religious movement. Through Christ men see for the first time in history a perfect personality, and through Christ, men's sins are all redeemed.

For a personality as great as Christ to be revealed in the world gives meaning to the existence of the great multitude of human beings, loaded with imperfections as we are.

There are not lacking those to say that for the love of the one man, Christ, to redeem the sins of billions of others is incomprehensible. But in Romans 5:17, Paul says: " If one man's offense made death reign through that one man, all the more will those who receive God's overflowing mercy and his gift of righteousness live and reign through the one individual Jesus Christ." One is enough. By the sin of one, billions have been made sinners, and now salvation for all comes through one great personality. But this doctrine is unintelligible from the materialistic point of view — from the numerical standpoint — whether of algebra, arithmetic or geometry. Considered psychologically, as a spiritual matter, it can be grasped. As the degeneracy of one man spread to all peoples, all are saved through the salvation vouchsafed by One. Since we are dealing in terms of love, the numerical demands of God's algebra can all be satisfied through the love of One man. Through the appearance of a person like Christ, God is satisfied. Christ is the summit of evolution; and so when the one perfect One, Christ, is revealed, all the disappointments of the past are redeemed.

Next is the phenomenon of degeneration. " If the first handful of dough is consecrated, the whole mass is, and if the root of a tree is consecrated, so are its branches. If some of the branches have been broken off, and you who were only a wild olive shoot have been grafted in, in place of them, and made to share in the richness of the olive's root, you must not look down upon the branches. If you do, remember that you do not support the root; the root supports you." (Romans 11:16–18.) Paul is illustrating his theme with reference to the process of grafting. Paul seems to have known intimately this business of grafting. In Kishu province I have heard a saying: " If the root is good, even the fruit is changed through it." If a Japanese tangerine be grafted onto a Bengal quince root, the root will influence the tangerine tree and make it a quince. This was the thing that Paul was speaking of. Ordinarily we think the root of no account and that it is the fruit alone which is important.

Great energy is released in the tree when it is grafted.

Even though it may be so old as to be decrepit, a plum tree with a new branch grafted on becomes much stronger. In Ika there are many famous old plum trees, from one hundred to three hundred years old, and even those which have been reduced to nothing but bark and branches, when grafted, are astonishingly strengthened. When lilies are cross-fertilized sometimes their strength comes back completely. Even when we are completely exhausted, if we become joined to Christ, power arises in a wonderful way from within us. When we keep ourselves on the strong foundation which is Christ, life overflows within us. Energy steadily arises in even such feeble creatures as we are when we lay hold of Christ. That which I felt I could not possibly accomplish turns out very well. Shrewd and selfish people, when they receive Christ's spirit, get to living unselfish loving lives.

THE PARABLE OF THE GO-BETWEEN

We ourselves so often fail to choose definitely between good and evil. Undecided between God and man, we do not cling to God very well, nor yet to man, and so come to our wits' end with indecision. Speaking of this dilemma, Paul said, " Wretched man that I am, who shall deliver me from the body of this death! " But through the Cross of Christ we can return to the righteous path: " We actually glory in God through our Lord Jesus Christ, to whom we owe our reconciliation." (Romans 5:11.) " Through your union with Christ you who were once so far away have through the blood of Christ been brought near." (Ephesians 2:13.)

Through Christ we come near to God. Christ is our go-between. " I don't need a Christ. It is quite possible for me to come to God directly," says someone. To such a one I would say, " You may think that an evidence of your superiority; but when the essence of love becomes a little clearer to you, you will understand that one enters into fellowship blessing for the first time through a mediator."

People who are steeped in the thought of the nineteenth and twentieth centuries are not fond of this idea of a mediator. They deny the religion that places a mediator between themselves and God. But in the world of human beings, love has developed gradually. Because of all sorts of obstacles it has not evolved as it should. We are not able to oppose sin completely. Through the man who has really experienced God's love, love is being perfected. The facts of history teach us that men have to place something between themselves and God in order to be able to reach up to him. It is well to make Christ our guide to God. It is necessary to have a go-between for love. Even children, when they want something, do not ask their father directly, but ask through their mother or a friend. In personal relationships, it most often makes for good relationships for someone to stand between. It is so in marriage. And at the time of the Russo-Japanese war, it was when Roosevelt stepped in between Japan and Russia that the settlement was reached. When a go-between is established, things are carried along smoothly in a wonderful way.

Even in the realm of animals and plants there are many go-betweens. Parasites enter the human body through fishes. This is the law of the universe. We do not go to God directly but through Christ. We pray through Christ, but that does not refer merely to the Christ who died nineteen hundred years ago. It means that we pray believing in the love of God as revealed in Christ. A mediator is necessary for conciliation to occur in a labor strike. And for both sides to be willing to make concessions it is absolutely necessary to have the standard of love. Christ is the conciliator between God and man.

Through offering his body, Christ annulled the law, and acquitted us of the charges against us. This is a sublime idea, excellently depicted in the fifth, sixth and seventh chapters of Romans. Christ nailed selfishness to the Cross. The source of selfishness is instincts gone astray, and the cause of such derailment of the instincts is in the flesh. Christ crucified that flesh and nailed to the Cross all the sins of the human race.

Paul was penitent before God. He had held Christ in contempt, had arrested Christ's disciples, and had enjoyed the spectacle of the death of Stephen. All this was unpardonable — but Christ's death was a death to save *him*. So similarly the whole human race could be acquitted from its sins.

"What's this idiotic thing you are saying? It's unthinkable!" some of you may exclaim. But if you read the Bible you will understand it very well.

Christ could have escaped the Cross had he wanted to. So it is evident that he purposely chose the Cross. The Old Testament teaches that the Righteous One must surely die and that through this vicarious substitution, others will be acquitted. Christ believed that, and died in this spirit of the Old Testament. Moreover, if this had been attempted by an ordinary human being, it might have had no great effect. But since Christ was a person with a deep consciousness like that of God, since he died feeling the responsibility for the whole human race, this death becomes effective for all mankind.

There are many interesting traditions of vicarious substitution in the popular tales of the Tokugawa period, "The Rise and Fall of the Gempei." Christ died not for one person, however, but believing that he was dying for

the whole human race. So God, out of consideration for
that profound and lofty consciousness, does indeed forgive
the whole human race. Through the broad love of Florence Nightingale the Red Cross movement began and the
lives of a great number of pitifully wounded soldiers have
been saved. Christ's consciousness of deep love has
worked and become redemptive for the whole human
race. To those who believe this, Christ's Cross is indeed
the guarantee of the love of God. " For to those who are
on their way to destruction, the story of the Cross is nonsense, but to us who are to be saved, it means all the power
of God." (I Corinthians 1:18.)

THE PARABLE OF ADOPTION

Lastly, Paul explains that Christ's redemption makes
sinners the adopted sons of God, God's heirs. Together
with Christ we are made sons. If sons, then heirs.
" Heirs of God and fellow-heirs with Christ." (Romans
8:17.) The purpose of man's life is to become an in-
heritor or successor to God. Because Christ accepted and
adopted us sinners, though deep in our sins, we are redeemed and made God's sons. This was the final conclusion. This became possible through the love of Christ.
From whatever obscure origin a foundling may come,
he is an heir of God. Suppose a messenger should come
from the Iwasaki family with the word that you were to
be made its heir! But we can become heirs of God, who
owns the universe! The universe is said to have thirty
billion stars around the sun, and about twenty billion of
these in the Milky Way. The immensity of this starry
universe is the measure of the love of Christ.

Blood makes one bright and blooming, fresh and youth-
ful. Christ's blood makes us new again. It made the
prodigal son over into an heir of God.

Thus Paul uses parables to set forth his meaning. Starting from the parable of sin as crime leading to death, he next explains the soul's struggle using the illustration of military strife between opposing forces; then speaks of the redemption needed after commercial losses; or else the gardener's work of grafting; then sets forth the work of the priest as go-between or mediator; the next step is the sinner's being declared "not guilty" before the law; and last of all, he uses the parable of adoption as a son into the family. This ascending series of illustrations fits the fundamental values of Life — Power, Change, Growth, Selection, Law and Aim or Purpose. Borrowing the typical phenomena of many aspects of human society — the courts of justice, the military service, business, agriculture, the temple and the family — Paul associates them all in a statement of the process which saves all through love. He shows how God is blessing the believer through all the manifold pathways of his life. The reality of the love of Christ redeems the past, the present, and the future.

PRAYER

Father God: We thank Thee that Thou didst vouchsafe the precious Cross of Christ for our redemption. We are too likely to forget Thy limitless love, to cower because of our weakness, to think merely of the past. Enable us to be more clearly assured of the Redemption of the Cross and thereby more filled with energy for loving service. To this end, that we may be more clearly shown the meaning of the Cross, we pray humbly through Christ. Amen.

VII

THE CROSS AS TRUTH

To sum up all things in Christ, the things in the heavens, and the things upon the earth; in him, I say, in whom also we were made a heritage, having been foreordained according to the purpose of him who worketh all things after the counsel of his will; to the end that we should be unto the praise of his glory, we who had before hoped in Christ: in whom ye also, having heard the word of the truth, the gospel of your salvation — in whom, having also believed, ye were sealed with the Holy Spirit of promise. Ephesians 1:10-13.

THE CROSS is the secret of Christianity. The truth of the Cross fascinates the hearts of men, says Paul. He insisted that though it might seem to be a seductive teaching, yet it is really the truth. It was the Greeks' calling the Cross a piece of superstition that led to this emphasis on his part. Today, too, there are those who ask, " Where is the truth in the Cross? "

There are many types of truth — natural truth, physiological truth, psychological truth, and rational truth. The electric light glows, a book falls to the floor — these are instances of natural law, or truth. Flowers bloom in order that plant life may develop; this is fulfilment of purpose. There is truth in a clock telling the time. In the case of certain machines, natural truth gives way to a higher type of truth. A clock, made according to the laws of physics, and therefore demonstrating the truth of physics, becomes also an instrument for measuring time and thus illustrates a higher type of truth. Our bodies exist as a result of many scientific modifications, and reveal physiological truth in that they sustain life; but at the same time they also demonstrate psychological truth. In all natural law we discover truth, for it is everywhere, in the soil, and in the beauty all about us.

The whole universe is divine. Its perfection lies in that it is ever advancing along one path. This is the meaning in Christ's words, " I am the Way, the Truth, and the Life." Paul says Christ is the Head of the universe. (Colossians 1:18.) This means the perfection of the universe. He is the Head of a Divine Social Order. The human race cannot produce a fitting social order without the appearance of perfect personalities like that of Christ. If we regard Christ as the Head of such an order, love becomes an essential in the building of that order and sacrifice is the necessary foundation of love. The Cross is sacrifice made thoroughly conscious, and willed at every point. Therefore, though the Cross may seem to be false, yet it exists for the fulfilment of the universe.

The Cross completes the truth of natural law. If the universe is to be brought to perfection, mankind must be perfected; and in order to bring mankind to perfection, it is necessary to perfect love. In order to bring love to perfection, we must bring the Cross to perfection. It is not foolish to make the Cross our symbol. We find profound meaning in the words of Paul in Colossians: " For it was the good pleasure of the Father that in him should all the fulness dwell, through the blood of his cross." (Colossians 1:19-20.) What, then, is the meaning of the blood of the Cross?

THE SEVEN BASIC ELEMENTS OF TRUTH

We find seven essential elements in the truth of the Cross. In the first place, the Cross restores *life* by redeeming or making amends for sin. In order to give life, it is necessary to give the blood, which is the foundation of life. We can say that blood brings recovery to life, because life is supported or sustained by blood.

The second point is *power*. The powers of darkness have made sinners their slaves, and we must wrest them out of the hands of these powers through the power of Christ.

The third point is *change*, or transformation. We must lead men out of confusion back into the straight way. There are times when we are perplexed, and there are times when we see our way clearly. There are times when we would go straight to our goal, yet we do not see the way.

The fourth point is *growth*, or development. Although man is facing God, yet mankind is not stretching up on tiptoes in his effort to grow up to God. All the time one should be becoming more and more like God, yet one stops short on the way. Thus sin is arrested development. It was for this reason that God allowed Christ to die, just as a grain of wheat, when planted, is left to die. By becoming a seed, and dying for the sake of the entire human race, he bears fruit a hundred and a thousand-fold. This method of sacrifice by death is the only true way of progress.

The fifth point is *selection*, or cleansing. The crippled, and those who were considered to be of no account — these were the ones Christ called to him. In one of his parables Christ tells us how, when a banquet was to be given, the host first thought he would invite the best people, but when they would not come, he gave orders to bid those who were counted the most worthless folk in the world. We would be apt to invite only the learned, the upper classes, those of position and fame, but Christ did not look at it that way. Christ does not call the perfect; he calls those who are imperfect. " They that are whole have no need of a physician, but they that are sick. I came not to call the righteous but sinners." (Matthew 9:12–13.) Those in the church are those who realize they are " sick." Christ chooses these imperfect people in order that he may make them perfect.

The sixth point is *law*. That is, the sinner is to be saved through the truth. The seventh point is *purpose;* that is, the redemptive purpose of God, shown in the bringing back of the prodigal son.

Christ used many parables but these seven essential elements are to be found in any one of them. The reason that we do not understand the Cross is because we do not grasp these points. When we analyze the Cross as the foundation principle of life, we discover these seven points, and we can easily grasp the meaning of the various parables and figures of speech which Christ uses when we apply this analysis to them. In this way the ideas of Christ and of Paul become clear and intelligible to us.

Paul, in explaining the Cross, used a figure of speech which would attract the attention of merchants. He likened the transformation of Christian conversion to the process of barter and explained that redemption was one of the underlying principles of barter or exchange. He talks of buying back something which you have sold. At another time he uses the figure of a peace being declared between armies which have been fighting each other on the field of battle. Again he uses the figure of a person acting as a mediator for those who have been dragged into court. Again he uses the illustration of the priest offering sacrifices in the temple, and likens the suffering of Christ on the cross to this rite. Thus Paul uses figures of speech drawn from all walks of life.

There must be a transformation in the human soul as it progresses along the path from being a man to becoming a God. It requires strength to become a child of God. It becomes essential to choose one's path. Life consists in making these choices; one develops by choosing. Christ satisfies the hungry soul, saves the sinner, and redeems. Paul uses the term " righteousness " to describe this change. From the standpoint of the law, it is necessary to clear the offender of guilt. In order to make men his own children, God calls them out, chooses them, and makes them his heirs, " meet to be partakers of the inheritance of the saints in light." (Corinthians 1:12.) God, in order to make us into his children has to make us grow, little by little, and he makes us develop by redeeming us by his blood and clearing us of guilt.

THE FOREKNOWLEDGE OF THE CROSS

We must now consider the blood of Christ, that is, the Cross, as the principle of truth. We must think of the blood of the Cross as salvation. Christ was continually referring to blood in his teaching. At the Last Supper he said, " This is my blood of the covenant," and taking the bread in his hands, " This is my body." Blood and bread are elements which sustain life. Jesus said, " Greater love hath no man than this, that a man lay down his life for his friends." (John 15:13.) Long before he spoke these words, Jesus had been pondering the thought of offering his blood and of rending his flesh for the sake of giving life. These words did not fall from Jesus' lips as a sudden unpremeditated utterance.

From the very beginning of his public ministry of three years, Christ used the figure of blood in his teaching. Perhaps the words of John the Baptist, " The Lamb that beareth the sins of the world," had sunk deeply into his mind. In any case, we find this idea appearing even in the Sermon on the Mount. He tells his hearers, " You will certainly have to sacrifice yourselves; you will have to suffer." He speaks of the day when the bridegroom will be taken from among them; by this he meant the Cross. Although in some ways Christ was like a bridegroom, splendid and brilliant, yet beneath the surface there was loneliness. When Christ said that a greater event would take place than any which had happened in the time of Jonah, he meant the Cross. Over and over again Christ alluded to the Cross. From the time that John the Baptist was killed, he declared clearly that he would be sentenced to death, and finally die upon the Cross.

From the very first, therefore, Christ was conscious of the Cross. Strange as it may seem to us, the path which Christ was to tread was clearly revealed in the Scriptures. Christ believed and accepted all that is thus revealed in the holy writings, and often reasoned with his disciples in some such words as these: "Haven't you read the teachings? Isn't it written in the Scriptures that righteous men must inevitably suffer and those who are the saviors of the people are, without exception, put to death? "

Christ thus emphasized the important points of his teaching — the offering of blood, the rending of the flesh, the setting up of the standard of love. In order to bestow life, it is necessary to offer one's life blood. He made it plain what he meant by losing one's life through the figure of the blood.

THE CROSS AS THE PRINCIPLE OF TRUTH

Let us consider the Cross from three aspects. First, the Cross is implied in the principle of social solidarity. When one part of society suffers, we all suffer. The responsibility for society rests upon us all; this is the horizontal aspect of the Cross. We are all compelled to sacrifice for society. This is the principle of truth in the Cross, or the figure of blood shed for another. Second, there is no stepping upward from one level to the next, without sacrifice. One generation must sacrifice for the succeeding generation. This we may call the perpendicular aspect of the Cross. This is the inner meaning of Jesus' parable of the grain of wheat. The mother, in order that her child may grow, must sacrifice her own sleep at night to care for him. If she does not do this, the child does not develop as he should.

Christ declared that just as the principle of development was eternal, so there must be an eternal offering of blood, an eternal sacrifice. This is an eternal principle of truth. From the standpoint of the whole creation, no matter how worthless or unclean a life some human beings may be living, yet because they are included within the whole, we must improve their condition or the whole body will become infected. If one's little finger is injured, unless the blood circulates freely to the very tip of the finger, the whole body will suffer. It becomes imperative to God to save all men, even the most worthless. A revolution of force has as its aim the elimination of ignoble lives, but the gospel movement insists that we must save them. This is the spirit of the Cross of Christ. The God of the Universe is not some vague and indefinite Being, the Absolute, the Infinite, cold and unfeeling. God is love. The fathomless love of the universe is revealed in Christ. To redeem others by one's blood, to fear no suffering, to disregard death, to sacrifice everything, pressing forward with boldness toward the goal — these principles of the truth of the Cross, are found the very nature of God. The Cross is the crystallized love of God.

Therefore Paul cries, " Far be it from me to glory, save in the Cross of our Lord." And again, " For the word of the Cross is to them that perish, foolishness, but unto us who are being saved, it is the power of God." Again and again Paul reiterates that we must live the Cross. In Colossians he says, " Now I rejoice in my sufferings for your sake, and fill up on my part that which is lacking of the afflictions of Christ in my flesh for his body's sake, which is the church." Like soldiers charging the enemy, we must press forward, bearing the Cross of Christ.

The world progresses. Christ died two thousand years ago but still his work is not complete. We must still fill up what is lacking in his work. We must share in redeeming the ever recurring sin of man. We must become like Christ. By experiencing the love of Christ ourselves, and bearing his Cross together, we must further the progress of the world. In Philippians we find the words, " To suffer on behalf of Christ." That is, to participate in his suffering. If we take up this Cross and go forward, the world will advance and make progress; without the Cross, the world will never be perfected. This is what I call the principle of truth in the Cross.

PRAYER

O God our Father: We thank Thee for Thy great plan through which blood was shed upon the Cross in order to save us. We thank Thee that Thou didst reveal to our gaze the priceless blood of the Cross, to us who are so slow of heart, so unable to grasp Thy aims. We are still unable to fully comprehend the meaning of the blood which Christ shed for us, and are following our own wilful ways, while the world gropes on in darkness. Oh, cause us once more to experience afresh the eternal truth of the Cross. Drive us forward into the world, to shoulder its burden of suffering and pain. Wipe away, we beseech Thee, all the sins of the world through the blood of the Cross. In the name of Christ. Amen.

VIII

THE CROSS AND THE BLOOD OF CHRIST

But if we walk in the light, as he is in the light, we have fellowship one with another, and the blood of Jesus Christ his Son cleanseth us from all sin. I John 1:7.

"THIS IS my blood of the covenant which is poured out for many unto remission of sins," said Jesus. In these words he taught us that this blood had a direct relation to the salvation of the human race. It is clear that Christ had this conception from the time of his early ministry in Galilee. Paul accepted this idea and also regarded the blood of Christ as indispensable for the salvation of mankind. "God set forth Jesus to be a propitiation through faith in his blood." (Romans 3:25.) We find the same thought in Peter, as for example in I Peter 1:18, 19: "Knowing that ye were redeemed with precious blood, even the blood of Christ." This was also the faith of Christ's disciple John.

Why is it that Christ and also his disciples believed that there was a special connection between the salvation of mankind and the blood of Christ? In the history of religion, we find that there has been that connection from earliest times. In the nomadic period before agriculture was developed, a sheep was man's most valued possession, and by far the most precious part of the sheep was its blood. Thus the blood of the sheep came to be the most precious offering which mankind could make God and to have a supremely solemn and sacred meaning.

THE SHEDDING OF BLOOD AND EMANCIPATION

On the night when the Hebrew people were to be rescued out of slavery in Egypt, God commanded that a sprinkling or smear of blood be placed upon the doorposts of their dwellings. It was no accident that blood should thus become the mystic symbol of the freeing of the Jewish people and should be kept in memory by the Festival of the Passover. The name "Passover" was given this festival because the angel passed over the houses on whose doorposts there was a sprinkling of blood. It was a time when the Jewish people gave expression to their devotion and complete submission to God by bringing him their most precious possession and joyfully flinging it down at his feet. Thus the belief was deeply impressed upon their hearts that as blood was indispensable for the freeing of their people from slavery, so it was also necessary for the freeing of the soul from sin. As a primitive people they had no philosophy, but they felt that blood was necessary to life, and therefore blood became a symbol of life.

THE STRANGE POWER OF BLOOD

Blood has a strange power. First, it cleanses the body of impurities, draws away the pus from injured tissues and restores them. Second, it even has the power of re-building tissues that have been destroyed. It builds not only skin and flesh, but, as in the case of the fingernail, it has the mysterious power of reproducing the structure and form as well. Third, the blood has the power of controlling the development of any part of the body, a power which reaches into the future.

Thus with the soul as well as the body. The blood not only brings redemption from sin but has the power to bring about development even to the point where a man feels himself to be a child of God. This conception of the mysterious power of blood was evidently that of Christ and his disciples. But the theological scholars of the nineteenth century were too rationalistic and rejected it. They did not see religion as related to life. They thought of the soul as an abstraction. But the soul does not exist apart from life.

The power of blood means the power of love! If blood can bring recovery to the sores of the body, love has the power to redeem the wounds of the personality. If blood has the power to restore broken-down tissues, love can make the wounded personality whole again, until it becomes a child of God. It is the teaching of the New Testament that the sacrificial love of Christ has this power to redeem and make restitution for all the past sins of humankind. Not that physical blood can redeem the sins of the soul; but to love other men enough to be willing to pour out your blood for them, this is the acme of spiritual love. Such love has the power to redeem and in this lies the hidden reason why Christ poured out his blood upon the cross.

The scholars of the nineteenth century could not understand how Christ could die as a substitute for man, but for Christ and his disciples the concept of a substitute contained no difficulty. In Matthew 20:28 we find Christ saying, " The Son of Man came to give his life a ransom for many." Here the blood of Christ, that is, of one individual, is regarded as the indemnity or reparation which saves many souls. In a previous chapter we noted that old question, raised perhaps by the brethren of the first Christian community, " How can one individual become the salvation of many? " and the attempt in the fifth chapter of Romans to answer it through the law of inheritance. The circulation of the blood in the human body, however, provides a sufficient explanation. The action of blood is universal; it functions throughout the body, feeding the nerve tissues, the digestive organs, the bones, the muscles and circulating throughout the whole system, having the power to restore any part of it. It is the same with love. Love is endowed with the power to redeem and heal throughout the past, present and future, every part of the whole. The supreme manifestation of that love is the blood which Christ shed on the Cross. We believe it to be the manifestation of his love and are enabled to believe in the forgiveness of past sins and the healing of past offences.

THE SOURCE OF FUTURE LIFE

But the blood not only heals past sins; it also gives fresh hope to those who are crippled, and who long to become whole again. God forgives all the failures of mankind, throughout all the past, out of consideration for Christ's sacrifice. The ransom which Christ paid is not a price paid for redemption alone. For the sake of redeeming mankind, he has also met the responsibility of the human race towards God. We have allowed the debt we owe to God to go unpaid; some kind of effort is necessary to recall us, who have wandered away, to the right path, and to restore us to our true selves. This effort — an effort so great it thrills us — Christ himself put forth. This price which Jesus paid is like the work of the blood in healing old wounds. It is a costly work. The blood surrenders itself as a sacrificial ransom, fully and freely pouring itself out for the sake of the injured part of the body. So Christ died that others might be resurrected into new life.

Through the recovery afforded by this love-pattern, mankind is thus granted the possibility of being restored once more to the status of a child of God. Faith in this possibility is indeed faith in God. This is wholly the gift of Christ for there is no reason, apart from his love, why faith towards God should spring up in our hearts.

When Christ poured out his blood upon the Cross, he set mankind an example before God. To the extent to which mankind shows forth love of this sort, it becomes unnecessary for the God of heaven and earth to seek for a more perfect manifestation of love. If human beings advance to the point of pouring out their life blood for others, they are then fully restored, fully recovered.

We cannot doubt that the blood of the Cross is the purest and most precious blood ever shed in all history. This is the blood which is to save mankind, to redeem sinners, and make the human race into children of God. The world has seen much shedding of blood, blood shed for private advantage, or to satisfy selfish desires. But the blood which Christ shed was to save mankind. This blood is life itself. "With a spear they pierced his side, and there came out blood and water," writes John in his Gospel, and the words are full of deep meaning. For nineteen centuries this blood has been the fountain of life and healing for the souls of countless millions. We appreciate anew the lines of the hymn which William Cowper sang:

> "There is a fountain filled with blood,
>   Drawn from Emmanuel's veins."

Through this blood-stained love which gave up life itself, we must receive the forgiveness of all our past sins, and the healing of all the wounds of our hearts. Through this marvelous fountain of Emmanuel's blood we are to

accept healing from all sin — sins which others see, and
sins they cannot see — our individual sins, and the sins of
society.

PRAYER

Our Father in Heaven: We thank Thee that through the
blood which Thy son Jesus Christ shed upon the Cross, all
the old wounds and injuries of our hearts are healed and
we are cleansed. We praise Thee that it has been made
plain that no matter how great our sin, it is possible for us
to be wholly saved. We are deeply grateful, Lord, that
whether shut within prison walls, we grieve over the sin of
murder, or whether appalled by the horror of the sins we
have committed, we stumble out in the forests of the
mountains, we can believe that through the precious blood
shed on Calvary's mount, we can once more be made into
men. Our sins and offenses are not Thy responsibility,
nor the fault of society. They are the mistakes which we
have made through our own selfishness and careless con-
duct. We thank Thee that Christ revealed such tremendous love towards us sinners. We believe in Thy great
love, and taking Thee simply at Thy word, unworthy as
we are, we accept Thy salvation and are born anew. With
our eyes filled with tears of thankfulness, we can only
long for Thy love and come home to Thy bosom. Amen!
Amen! We offer up our praise before Thee for the merit
of the Blood of the Cross.

IX

THE CROSS AND PRAYER

*My father, if it be possible, let this cup pass away
from me; nevertheless, not as I will, but as Thou wilt.*
Matthew 26:39.

THE LAST week of Christ's life was dramatic. Even in
the Gospel of Mark, the record of these days is full and
long. The events in the garden of Gethsemane are described in detail in the Fourth Gospel. (John 16, 17.)
It tells us that after his last talk with his disciples, Christ
" went forth with them over the brook Kedron." In Matthew we are told that " when they had sung a hymn, they
went out into the Mount of Olives." Every year a great
festival is held in Palestine to celebrate the deliverance of
the Hebrews from slavery. It is probable that the hymn
which Christ sang as he and his disciples crossed the
brook Kedron was the song sung at this festival, a song
of praise. Christ was composed and calm enough to sing,
although he realized that Judas was laying a plot against
him. No doubt he felt, as he entered that garden, that he
had been singing his own funeral dirge.

When you visit Palestine today, and cross the brook
Kedron, you find a road on the bank opposite the garden
of Gethsemane, which in former days probably led from
the Gate Beautiful to the garden. Nowadays this road
is closed, and one has to enter from the northern side, but
it is possible that Christ entered the garden by this road

from the Gate Beautiful. In those days there were many olive trees growing in the garden. Probably Christ left his disciples, and went on by himself a few paces to pray beneath some large tree. He must have prayed aloud, for otherwise there would have been no way for us to know of the prayer in the 38th and 39th verses of Matthew. It was a very short prayer, and it was overheard, no doubt, by the disciples a little distance off.

THE NIGHT OF SORROW

Although Christ seldom revealed his heart to others, this night he said, " My soul is exceeding sorrowful, even unto death." This was plain speaking for Christ. It was as though he said to Peter, " I am so burdened with anxiety that I feel as though I were going to die." His emotion was heroic, and far beyond the imagination of the ordinary man. The disciples had no occasion for dejection. Up to the very last moment they thought that if Christ would simply raise his hand, he could take over the government of the country; therefore they felt that there was no reason for anxiety. Christ's saying that he was burdened with anxiety, even to the point of death, reveals the tremendous difference between his point of view and theirs. Christ was not anxious about the possibility of revolution or about how to control the people in case of such an uprising; he was burdened by his sense of responsibility for the fate of humankind.

It was this that made Christ pray with such earnestness. He was in distress of mind as to whether or not he should seek to avoid the fate which he had taken upon his shoulders. " My Father, if it be possible, let this cup pass away from me; nevertheless, not as I will, but as Thou wilt." It was a brief and simple prayer, yet it clearly revealed Christ's feelings.

Three groups of people were there that night. First, Christ and his best loved disciples; second, the eight other disciples; third, the chief priest and his servants, and Judas Iscariot, who had been in treacherous communication with them. Before leaving the house Christ had foretold that his fate was drawing near.

As he entered the garden he may have heard the sound of footsteps approaching. He was fully aware of what was happening. Telling his disciples to " watch and pray," he went to pray himself. His disciples were tired and fell asleep. More than once he returned to them to warn them, but they were too tired even to reply to him.

As he prayed in agony he could hear the tramp of the feet of those bent on his destruction. They drew nearer and nearer. As they came up to him, Christ said, " Behold, he is at hand that betrayeth me." He knew Judas Iscariot was the man. Judas knew the place to which he was likely to go. Only about a week before that, Christ had chosen this garden as a place of prayer. The records tell us that he went frequently to the Mount of Olives. That was why Judas came to look there for him. He knew it would not be hard to find him. If not in the garden, it would be easy to find him by inquiring of Martha and Mary in Bethany.

" Friend, for what purpose have you come? " was Christ's response as Judas kissed him. An instant later that purpose was abundantly clear, for the soldiers seized Jesus. Impetuous Peter indignantly attacked them, cutting off the ear of the high priest's servant. Jesus reproved him and healed the man; then meekly yielded himself to his captors and left the garden.

A WHOLLY HUMAN CHRIST

There was a custom in Egypt and Asia Minor of giving condemned criminals a cup of poison to drink. Christ did not wish to drink this bitter cup of the Cross and yet chose it. It would have been easy for him to have chosen his own happiness instead of God's great mission for him, but he did not seek ease. His whole life was freed from self and given to seeking to do God's will.

We see the Christ-likeness of Jesus in his repeated prayer, " Thy will be done." Had he only said, " Thy will be done," it would not have been a prayer. It is the words, " Let this cup pass away from me," which make it a true prayer. It is a human prayer, and yet it breathes a spirit of complete consecration. " If the Cross is necessary, make me, I beseech Thee, take Thy way; I have no desires or hopes of my own; if there is no other way, I accept Thy will gladly." Here we see the point of struggle in Christ's experience. If he had been so far separated from human feelings as to say merely, " O God, do as Thou wilt," it would not have been genuinely human suffering. He is human because as one who was to manifest God's will upon earth, he was caught in a dilemma, and his nobility lies in the way he met this dilemma. Herein, too, lies the greatness of our religion.

There are two ways of looking at the problem, God's way, and man's way. According to the human viewpoint, one wishes to map out his own road; but when he considers God's will he throws aside his selfishness, and becomes willing to follow God's path. The prayer at Gethsemane is the bond between these two. From the human standpoint, one is averse to the Cross; one does not wish to inflict death on one's self; but from God's viewpoint, this is unavoidable. To choose death seems like a self-contradiction; but when we really make up our minds to pray, there is no other prayer but this.

Inasmuch as the depth of one's religious experience is measured by the degree to which God can use one accord-

ing to his purposes, it becomes profoundly significant
to us that Christ should have offered such a prayer. The
majority of people, both in former times and in this present day, take the attitude that the inevitable is God's will.
But that is not Christ's attitude; up to the very last moment, he realizes he has the power of choice and yet he
accepts God's will. Herein we see Christ's true character.

There are many of us Orientals who say, " It is God's
will! " It is an old saying with us that everything is
karma; everything is determined by fate. But that is
equivalent to saying that man is not free to choose in any
situation; one may be fated to commit murder, or to die
by starvation; there is nothing we can do about it.
Christ's attitude, however, was that, as a human being,
he was free to choose and he was determined to live his
life to the full. He would exert himself to the utmost,
and then what man could not do must be left to the will
of God. Herein lies the focal point of Christ's spiritual
struggle.

THE ETERNAL GETHSEMANE

Christ did a glorious thing when he made restitution to
God. It was far above what other men would think of
doing. He felt a deep sense of responsibility, and was fully
conscious of the meaning of his act. It was not suicide;
but rather Christ revealed his true character when he
gravely chose that way. We must follow this same path;
after we have poured out every bit of human effort possible, then we must say, " Let it be done according to
God's will." This is the eternal Gethsemane.

Charles Gordon was the British general who came to
China, and later died in battle at Khartoum in Egypt. It
is said that when Gordon prayed, he put a white handkerchief at the entrance to his tent. When that white

handkerchief was flying, no one was permitted to enter, for it was his time for prayer. He persevered in prayer, and he did not pray merely about his own problems. He used to pray, " Deliver us, O Lord, if it be Thy will, from being surrounded by the enemy, but if there is no other way and my men must die, let them die as unto Thee." We must have this serious earnestness in prayer.

Marshal Foch is said to have been often in prayer. He used to pray continually during battle. If he had a moment to spare, he used to go to pray into some church, wrecked by shells, and gaping with shell-holes, for prayer was to him simply a form of guidance.

There is a lesson for us in the fact that Jesus prayed the whole night through. In long-continued meditation one draws nearer and nearer to God, until he makes his petitions not for the advancement of his own interests, but for the glory of God. The heavier the responsibilities one carries, the more numerous are the demands which one makes of God. The more one feels his own responsibilities, the more deeply should one ponder the prayer of Christ in Gethsemane.

In the early days of Christianity in Japan, there came a moment of crisis in 1873 when there was a general cry for the extermination of the new faith. There were but a handful of Christians when Ibuka, Uemura, Okuno, and a group who were living in Dr. Brown's school, received word from Tokyo that they would probably be killed. They thought their throats would be cut that very night. They met together and prayed earnestly not for escape, but that since they believed in the Cross, they might have the resolution to die upon it. In the midst of their prayer meeting, they received another communication that they had been pardoned. They were so full of joy, they hardly knew whether their heads were still on their shoulders or not. Our Christianity, Japan's Christianity, has come down to us from such a prayer meeting.

THE CROSS AS FATE

To us Orientals it is possible, as I said above, to think of the Cross as Christ's *karma*. Such Oriental determinism is, however, in complete contrast to the attitude of Christ. Through Christ's faith it was revealed to him that he could not selfishly protest against the Cross, and he prayed, " Take my life, if it be Thy will, but save me, if it be Thy will that my life should be spared." Someone has said that the work of atonement was accomplished in the Garden of Gethsemane rather than on the Cross. There is some truth in this. According to Luke's account, Christ prayed with such earnestness that his sweat became drops of blood. When we think of this impassioned prayer, we realize that we, too, must pray with like flaming earnestness for Japan, for America, for China, for the whole world. Not one such petition is in vain. Prayer is bound to be heard.

I am particularly struck with the fact that Christ's prayer was not in the least for himself. If prayer has meaning only for one's self, it will not be heard. True prayer is not for one's self. If it voices the aspirations of humanity, it will be heard. There was not the slightest trace of selfishness in Christ's prayer, " If for the redemption of mankind, it is necessary that I should be killed, I am willing to go to my death." This attitude is the acme of the life of faith. To pray in this spirit is the highest type of religious consciousness. When in poverty, distress, or any sort of trouble we pray in this spirit, we gain the victory.

Christ gave up his life upon the Cross the day after he prayed this earnest prayer. And there is proof that his prayer was answered, in that the men of the world have been drawn to him, and that even now a consciousness of the reality of Christ continues with us; a consciousness so deep and satisfying that it is fully adequate to our needs.

We do not have enough conviction about prayer. If we pray only a little, our prayers are answered only to that degree. If we pray much, we receive many answers. Christ's activity was founded on prayer. We must not make ourselves alone the center, but our prayers must show a sense of responsibility toward God for Japan, for Asia, for the whole world.

PRAYER

Great God our Father: As we call to mind the scene of Christ's suffering in Gethsemane, our hearts are filled with penitence and shame that we foolishly waste our time in idleness and that we make no progress in the Christian life from day to day. We confess that during these nineteen hundred years, though the world has advanced in scientific knowledge, we have made but little progress in respect and reverence for our neighbors and in love towards our fellow-men. We are ashamed that war and lust flourish and grow more rampant every day. Forgive us for our cruel indifference to the Cross, and pardon us that like the bystanders of old, we merely stand and gaze in idle curiosity upon the piteous scene. O teach us, we beseech Thee, the good news of Thy forgiveness. Cause humanity, degenerate as it is, to live anew, and hasten the day when the whole world shall be born again.

Grant Thy healing power to those who suffer from poverty and distress; to those who suffer in industry; to the workers who suffer unjustly in the factories; to those who are entangled by the temptations of the stock market, and have lost themselves in the mad race for riches. Save the hundreds of thousands of unemployed and relieve Japan of the insecurity which prevails throughout its borders. Oh, take away the sufferings of this sinful world.

Thou Living God! Lay Thy hands afresh upon the Houses of Parliament and grant us a righteous government through Thy power. Have pity upon China which has suffered one tumult after another these many years, and stretch forth a saving hand toward those regions which suffer from famine. Look down in compassion on the sufferings of Russia, of Korea, of Europe, and cause the day to draw nigh when these lands shall live in Thy peace. Let the gospel of Christ take deep root among our brothers in Germany, England, France and America. Pour down Thy Spirit upon us, and wrap the world in flames of fire which, like Pentecost, shall awaken all the nations of the world.

Teach us the solemnity of the Cross. Bless the churches of Japan and strengthen their faltering feet and withered hands. Teach these churches to pray with such earnestness that they will shed tears of blood for the redemption of mankind. We pray this in the name of Him who hung upon the Cross, our Savior Jesus Christ. Amen.

THE CROSS AND THE FINE ART OF DEATH

*O death, where is thy victory? O death, where is
thy sting? The sting of death is sin; and the power
of sin is the law: but thanks be to God who giveth
us the victory through our Lord Jesus Christ.* I Corinthians 15:55–57.

PAUL'S path lay through the borderland between life
and death, and he often met the latter face to face. He
was nearly killed in the outskirts of Lystra; he was threat-
ened by lions in the arena of Ephesus; he barely escaped
with his life by being let down in the middle of the night
in a basket from the top of the wall of the city of Damas-
cus. Having been thus repeatedly forced to face death,
Paul bursts into a triumphant song of victory. Like a
general returning from successful conquest, he cries out
that victory has drunk down death. " Death is swallowed
up in victory! "

It was not so with most men of those ancient times.
Death was a fearful thing to them. Men spent their whole
fortunes in anticipation of it. The pyramids show this.
Even in Japan we have mausoleums which took more than
one generation to build, such as that of the Emperor Nin-
toku. The Mozushima tomb, the greatest in all Japan,
was begun while the Emperor was still living and completed just a little while before his death, requiring a period
of some twenty-five or thirty years. Today such monu-

ments would cost millions of yen. The pyramids also were built before the death of the one in whose honor they were erected. At Milan in Italy, there are hundreds of tombs which have cost five million yen apiece. Upon arrival at the railroad station, it is the thing to do to go immediately to see them. Nor is it unusual to find in any country, in America and Europe, in Mexico, Brazil, or Peru, instances of men who have spent the earnings of a lifetime upon erecting their tombs.

Paul was both a philosopher and an idealist, and the message which he gave to the world was one which even the great rulers of Alexandria had not been able to proclaim. Why did not Paul feel any fear or insecurity? The fundamental reason is to be found in his relation to Jesus Christ.

In the first place, Jesus Christ did not fear death. Some eighteen months before his death, he foretold it. " I shall die," said he, " in a short time, and my death will not be an ordinary one. I shall die by crucifixion and that crucifixion will be at the hands of foreigners." Though Jesus foresaw his death, he went straight on, facing it squarely. He was submissive and obedient to God's will. He felt that death was a necessary thing and that he had conquered it. Paul's words give expression to the same idea. Death is not something to be afraid of; under certain circumstances death is in itself victory.

Another point is found in the resurrection. Had Jesus Christ not risen from the dead, Christianity would not be what it is today. The resurrection — that is, the mysterious experience of a future life — revitalized history. It was the experience of fearlessly treading death under foot which caused Paul to say these words. Because Paul was a philosopher, he could not be satisfied with Jesus' simple attitude; he must construct a theory of the resurrection. He explains it at length in a beautiful passage, in such a way that we are able to grasp the truth.

He distinguishes between a body which dies and one which does not die. The simple body of flesh dies, but there is something which does not die, that is, the spiritual body. We are born with a physical body; we are resurrected in a spiritual body. Jesus is said to have appeared to his disciples after his death with a certain body. How could he appear before them in visible form, when the doors were fast shut? Paul conceives of a spiritual body which exists in space, and was convinced that while one was born with a physical body, one could be resurrected with a spiritual body. (I Corinthians 15:12–14.)

THE PHYSICAL BODY AND THE SPIRITUAL BODY

A desk or a glass has a physical substance, while electricity, although still physical, is quite different from these things. All atoms are made up of electrons. These molecular atoms do not have a physical body such as we are accustomed to think of. A physical substance has weight, hardness, and breadth or thickness, but one cannot conceive of the atom as having solidity. It has been discovered that an atom has a definite weight — a form of energy in motion. Science has shown within the last few years that the atom is produced by waves of energy and therefore that one can conceive of it as having some slight breadth or thickness, but not solidity. When we follow this line of reasoning a little further, and take the next step, we can conceive of a substance which would not have weight or solidity, but which would have only extension or breadth. This is therefore the spiritual body. It is this sort of body that we dream of. The people of our dreams do not have weight or solidity but they do have a shape. In this way, the world of electrical forces is different from what we imagine.

Outside of purely physical concepts, there are many things in the phenomena of the universe that are beyond our comprehension. Unquestionably one of these is the soul's progress from the physical to the spiritual body. We do not by any means know all that there is to be known about this. We find the words, " We shall all be changed." (I Corinthians 15:52.) This means a step forward. It is an instantaneous change. Like the change which takes place when the babe leaves the womb, we are transformed instantly into spirit.

GOD DOES NOT DESERT US

Paul makes the point also that God does not abandon mankind to the fate of death. If God were merely to leave him to die, there would be nothing more pitiable than man. This is the cry of the human heart. As Paul ponders this problem, he concludes: " And if Christ hath not been raised, then is our preaching vain, your faith is vain; ye are yet in your sins. If the dead are not raised, let us eat and drink, for tomorrow we die." If the dead depart abruptly and the spirit perishes, and that is all there is to it, there is nothing better for us to do than to eat and drink, says Paul, for mankind has only the pleasure of the present moment.

Materialism is no new thing; it was found even in those ancient days. The cult of Pythagoras which was popular in the lands bordering on the Mediterranean was a materialistic cult. From this group of materialists there developed hedonism, teaching that there was no necessity for self-control or sacrifice, for love or service; the essence of human life was selfishly to seek one's own pleasure, and to spend one's life in rioting to one's heart's content.

Life is not so simple as that. The famous Myers of England, who died some ten years ago, made a specialty of psychical research to prove the continuity of human life. Such men as Lombroso of Italy, who was a Marxist and followers of Straus, who in 1848 were materialists, afterward revised their materialistic assumptions. In another twenty-five years Marxism, too, may become spiritual, for the conviction that man has a soul is too strong to remain long suppressed.

Paul's position was not the crude materialism of Marx. Standing on the steps, as it were, of weight and solidity, he conceives of a spiritual body which has neither of these characteristics. As a solid substance can become fluid, and the fluid a vapor, so we may conceive of life changing from one form to another. I am convinced that we of the twentieth century are in a position to think deeply into this problem.

DEATH AND THE CONTINUITY OF LIFE

It is a fact in mathematics that if any quantity is transferred from one side of an equation to the other it is unchanged, but its plus sign becomes a minus or its minus sign a plus. There is a corresponding continuity to be observed in the world of life. In it we can find no example of anything developed by a long and continuous process up to a certain point, suddenly being broken off and vanishing into nothingness. Nor is this consistent with man's real nature. In human progress, when the development of the physical body comes to a stop, the spirit develops. In the spiritual nature, first and most important is the development of the intelligence; when the growth of the intelligence halts, the emotions develop; and when the emotions cease to grow, the development of the will begins. Myers went so far as to assert that in the world after death, the intelligence does not develop, but only the will, and Sir Oliver Lodge also held this opinion.

If we conceive of a "nothingness" in the life after death, the German philosopher Schopenhauer says, we must also conceive of a "nothingness" which preceded the conception and life in the mother's womb. If we are to bewail the nothingness of the future, why not bewail the nothingness of the past?

The God of the universe has under certain conditions created us out of "nothingness." If this is true, and nothingness should again claim us in the future, the God of the universe will again call us out from the void. In other words, nothingness is not the terminal point. As long as God is infinite, our souls are also immortal. The soul is not immortal independently of God, but because the infinite God is mindful of us; in that sense our souls are indestructible. It was for this reason that Christ, who had utter confidence in the Heavenly Father, said when on the cross, "Into Thy hands I commend my spirit." Christ did not have the least fear of death. His trust in God, the Father in heaven, had trampled it under foot. Herein lies the victory also of his disciples.

DEATH AND VICTORY IN LIFE

There is one thing in the world which does not die. The science of physics tells us that the energy which fills the universe is indestructible; it is universal. That which relies on God does not die. Since God made death, death must have some useful purpose, otherwise it would not have been necessary for God to have made it. It has the function of selection, and to the good man, it gives rest from labor. If we believe in the God who made death, we need have no doubts or need we fear death in the least.

" But when this corruptible shall have put on incorruption and this mortal shall have put on immortality, then shall come to pass the saying that is written, Death is swallowed up in victory." (I Corinthians 15:54.) Paul finishes his sentence with the word victory. Death is the victory of God. Although to man things look hopeless, something greater than man has conquered him, and from the standpoint of that conqueror, death is intelligible. Death was created by God; there is no reason therefore why those who believe God should fear death. Since God is the Absolute Infinite, there is no death with God. This is what is meant by death being swallowed up in victory, for death is victory.

By victory, he means God's victory. D'Annunzio speaks of the victory of death, but Paul is talking about the victory of God. God is victory itself, and because we are assured of the victory which is in him, we trample death beneath our feet.

My teacher, Mrs. Logan, fell ill with pneumonia and the doctor gave up all hope of recovery. She knew for a day before her death that she was going to die. She sang a hymn in farewell, and asked others to sing her favorite hymn; then she called the servant who had worked for her for twenty years, and said, " Take good care of your master, and be careful that he does not suffer from the lack of proper food. You must not weep for we will surely meet again." They told me that it was with such words as these that she fell asleep. She went forth into death as though she were taking a journey from Kobe to Tokyo. It seemed to me when I heard this from Dr. Logan that there could not have been a more beautiful and victorious death than this. Mrs. Logan had been praying for her physician, for he had said that he could not understand religious faith. And he made a confession of faith on the spot, asking that he be counted a Christian. I do not know of any more splendid death. This is the victory which is in God.

We may not be able to understand physics, or the creation of electrons, or again we may have no knowledge of spiritualism, but we can believe that God created death. Paul cried, " O Death, where is thy victory? " We, too, must prepare for death by believing, with full assurance of absolute victory, that Jesus, by bearing the cross, has conquered death.

PRAYER

O God our Father: There are those among us who refuse to take life seriously. Forgive us, Lord, that though we are born into this stern old world, and must some day come face to face with the solemnity of death, yet we are spending our days like spoiled children. But Thou didst conquer death through Christ. We believe that Thou hast trampled death under foot and vanquished it utterly. Enable us, when we come face to face with death, to pass through it with perfect composure, and to hold fast a firm faith as we go into the world of eternity. Grant that we may discover God's path in deepened experience, through our lives of poverty; make us like God in purity, in depth. We beseech Thee to guide our young men, make them strong; inspire them, and save the land of Japan through them. We pray this in Christ. Amen.

XI

THOSE WHO TAKE UP THE CROSS

*But Jesus said unto them, Ye know not what ye ask.
Are ye able to drink the cup that I drink? or to be
baptized with the baptism that I am baptized with?*
Mark 10:38.

"THE CROSS is out of date! In this new age a religion
based on suffering is no longer of value. It should be sup-
planted by one of joy and hope and optimism. A religion
based on pain is medieval and unsuited to our modern
minds!" Though there are "enlightened" folk who say
this, I do not agree with them. Progress involves sacrifice,
and sacrifice is the only road toward perfection. It is an
eternal necessity — the sacrifice of the parent for the
child, of the teacher for his pupils, of the seed for the sake
of the harvest.

We are more familiar with the necessity of such sacrifices in a vertical time-sequence — as of the older generation for the sake of the younger — than in their horizontal
aspect. Sacrifice needs to be all-inclusive. We must assume responsibility for others born in the same age as ourselves, for society as a whole.

When a group of people make a contract to borrow
funds, if one member in the contract fails, the next party
must assume the liability, and if he fails, then the remain-
ing parties to the contract must bear the responsibility.
This joint responsibility for society is what we mean by
social solidarity.

In the twelfth chapter of I Corinthians, the relation of the body to its members is used as an illustration of the mutual responsibility of people for one another. If there were nothing to hold the members of the body together, it could not function; so with society. If we are truly concerned about its progress, we must take responsibility for society as a whole.

In direct opposition to this, the tendency of Christianity in the eighteenth and nineteenth centuries was toward individualism. In contradistinction to love of society, the individualistic virtues of independence and liberty were stressed. Thence came the terrible social corruption of our modern day.

The Cross of Christ has therefore two chief values. In the first place, it has a value in time. "Except a grain of wheat fall into the earth and die, it abideth by itself alone." For eternal progress, eternal sacrifice is essential. One of the greatest of Christ's parables is that of the lost sheep. Then the Cross has also a value in space. These values are eternal principles for us. Those who are too selfish, and too much absorbed in their own satisfactions, cannot understand the meaning of the Cross. But for those who are striving to make society flawless in every aspect, the Cross is a universal principle.

Christianity has taken this Cross and without understanding its significance has explained atoning love as dogma. To those who are without love, it is naturally a difficult dogma. They do not understand what sort of life-principle love is. We must fix our gaze upon the Cross. And from the universal love revealed there, we must come to a sense of responsibility for the whole of society. This may seem simple, but its implications constitute a challenge as wide as the universe and as difficult to compass.

THREE STEPS IN THE CROSS

The work of Christ manifested itself in three ways: first in teaching; second in practice; and third, in consciousness. His teaching was that of love; his practice, the practice of love; and his consciousness that of the Cross. His teaching was great in itself, yet it would not have made him great if it had been unaccompanied by practice.

Gandhi is an advocate of non-resistance but there is a group among his followers who on occasion throw bombs. The early Christians were consistent. They stood for taking no indemnity for injury and were absolutely faithful to this principle. Jesus himself is an example, and his movement may be considered as an unsuccessful revolution based on the principle of non-resistance. It is said that one tribe of Christians refused to fight in self-defense and were completely wiped out. To a wonderful degree of loyalty, they put their religion into practice. Today the Korean Christians, in the same sort of situation, though pillaged of their money by the army, put the teachings of Christ into practice. This is sublime.

Nineteen hundred years ago the practice of non-resistance on the part of the early Christians made scarcely a ripple; the world was not influenced by it. But the fact that we must note here is rather that they were fully conscious of what they were doing. That consciousness does influence us greatly. We must show ourselves Christians in the details of daily life, even in the way we light the kitchen fire. We must practice our principles not only among ourselves but in our relations with other nations. If we do not have the consciousness that we are the children of the true God, we look at those of other nations with scorn, and say, " That fellow's a foreigner! " We must practice our Christian principles as Japanese in our relations to the Chinese.

Christ's basic principle, which he expressed in saying that we must love even the very least of men, did not arise from his teaching, neither did it come from his practice. It grew out of the fact that he had entered into the consciousness of God. The consciousness of atonement, that is, the conscious sharing of the atoning purposes of God, is not separate from the consciousness of God, or the consciousness of being a child of God. Whoever would bear responsibility for others must have sympathies broad enough to include the failures, the human derelicts. He has not entered into the consciousness of God who looks at some mean fellow whom society counts worthless, and says, " Oh, that fellow! He's hopeless; he's just a good-for-nothing! " The nearer to God we come, the more conscious we grow of our responsibility towards those worthless folk who are regarded as the very dirt under one's finger-nail. If we ask why it was that Christ always chose the worthless folk, it was because he possessed a one hundred per cent consciousness of God; he shared to perfection in his own consciousness the redemptive purpose of God.

The communists tell us that all that is needed to set the world right is to destroy the bourgeoisie, because they have taken possession of a large percentage of the wealth of society. A capitalist who possesses property is guilty of a crime and the communists intend therefore to kill him. In this the communists do not distinguish between men and property, though even in the eyes of the law these are differentiated. This disregard of the sacredness of human life hinges on lack of consciousness of atonement; they do not share the consciousness of God. Although they have grasped the communistic principles of the

Soviet intellectually, yet in their practice they are still
" American " (and capitalistic), as one of their own leaders has said. But the three — teaching, practice and consciousness — must work side by side, as they did in
Christ, and we must strive for a unity of these three aspects in our work.

THE REALIZATION OF THE LOVE OF THE CROSS

We must have clear and strong convictions of our mission of atonement; we must share in the purpose of God,
who seeks to redeem all. This is what I mean by becoming God-conscious. The disciples of Christ possessed this
consciousness, even from the first century of the Christian
era. In the second century we find the early Christians
spending their strength in nursing the victims of the
plague, even though they themselves contracted the dread
disease. The nursing of the sick is one of the noblest pro-
fessions, for it is an expression of the spirit of the Cross.
The founder of the first hospital was Gallicanus. Holding the rank of consul, he devoted all his fortune to setting
up a place for the sick. He nursed them with his own
hands and was eager to help everyone, even slaves. Our
Japanese word for hospital is written with the two ideo-
graphs meaning " place " and " sick," a place for the sick,
but that is not the real meaning of the word hospital. A
" hospital " means literally " a place where kindness is
shown." We are mistaken in calling it a place for sick
people.

In the Occident in these " places where kindness is
shown " the nurses often display greater nobleness of
character than the doctors, and are highly respected. It
is said that in England the automobiles will stop when they
meet a woman walking along the street in uniform of the
hospital of St. Thomas. There is the same attitude of

respect toward nurses in America as well. There is a statue of the nurse Edith Cavell, in Charing Cross in London, and at the foot of the statue are the words, "Patriotism is not enough." When the Germans were displaying the bitterest hatred toward the English, Edith Cavell nursed the enemy soldiers with great devotion; but this nurse, who was the very incarnation of love, was shot as a spy. England has honored her by erecting this statue, and nurses have been granted the privilege of sitting next in rank to the plenipotentiaries of all countries at public functions.

You do not find the nurses in England starting a movement for higher wages; there are no such things as strikes among the nurses there, nor among the doctors, nor among the grade school-teachers. I am sorry that the nurses of Japan have been so insistent in demanding higher rates of pay. If one is going to be the sort of nurse who is concerned about getting a salary, it is better not to become a nurse at all. The doctor has no right to refuse to come, no matter when he is called. The true Red Cross means that one cares for the sick whether one receives a salary or not. Let us think of nursing as a practical expression of the love of the Cross.

The fundamental principles of redemption are not contained in theology alone; they must be actualized in social ways. Dogma is useful as an explanation of love. I believe in the resurrection in the sense that the love of God makes the resurrection possible. And the meaning of the Virgin Birth is that God's love is capable of it. And so with the doctrine of the Trinity; it means that God is not only a transcendent God, but that he enters into relation with mankind, he even dwells within us, poor and weak as we are. In the Father lies the transcendency of God; in the Son, his manifestation; in the Holy Spirit, his imma-

nence — this is the meaning of the Trinity. For that
reason, if we reject the doctrine of the Holy Spirit, we are
greatly put to it to explain the love of God.

I believe in God's sense of responsibility for the whole
of society as redemptive love. This is the fundamental
principle in the love of God. God's deep love has got
into touch with mankind. Fundamentalism, therefore, is
only a partial explanation of the love of God, and Modernism sees only the surface and does not dig down to the
root of the matter. Here in Japan it is my earnest hope
that our young people may not be carried away by either
of these "isms." I do not want to emphasize theological
controversies. I hope that our young people may rather
give their whole energies to the realization of sacrificial
love as wide as the whole of society and as broad as the
entire universe. I pray that they may penetrate beneath
the surface agitations of doctrine and dogma to the great
underlying law of love.

Only those who are fully conscious can thoroughly
grasp the principle of love.* In the individual, this principle is manifested as the Cross. We must re-study the
meaning of the Cross from both the standpoint of theology
and that of science, and re-discover its meaning; then it
will be no longer a Cross for mere discussion, or a doctrine

* This refers to Dr. Kagawa's outline of human evolution (*cf.* page
136) as consisting of three stages: unconsciousness, semi-consciousness,
and the fully conscious stage. This concept appears frequently in his
pages, as in the poetical introduction, where he writes, "Then after a
long interval came to full consciousness," and "Christ is the first man to
awake to full consciousness of the Universe." His phrase, in the same
poem, "This full Cross-consciousness," means the same thing, as also
when he writes: "In the history of the human race there is needed the
creation of this Cross-consciousness, that is to say, the creation of the
inner life of its very soul." Dr. Kagawa's idea is that individuals awaken
to this stage of full consciousness variously. Some are awake, and some
are not yet so. — H. T.

which but partially explains its meaning. The Cross will be an inner experience, and our consciousness of the Cross will be realized in practice.

THE ROAD OF SELF-LIMITATION

The Cross, because it is the Cross, proceeds from the infinite to the finite. It originates in the heart of God but it takes the form of a human being, a man. There is an element of self-limitation in the Cross. Christ told his disciples not to go to the Samaritans nor to the Gentiles, but to the lost sheep of Israel. He told them to go to the lost Judeans, though they numbered but one per cent of the people. That means that we must choose our sphere of activity. Some must work for the proletariat, some for the farmer class. Some are to limit themselves to the work for those who earn their livelihood upon the sea. Some people are to limit their work to those who are ill. They do not go to those who are in health, but to those who are weak, to those who are "lost" through illness. We must dig deep in these limited fields of labor. As long as we are drawn hither and thither, and want to do this, and that, there is no Cross in it for us.

The worst limitation our Cross will put upon us will be personal weakness caught from our environment. If you go among the lost sheep, beware lest you yourselves should lose your way. It is the common mistake of elementary school-teachers that no matter where they go they think of themselves as teachers, and do not have the desire to be taught. When we go to work for the poor in the slums, we find them all talking roughly, and unconsciously, we too, before we know it, may have caught their rough way of speech.

Christ said a striking thing when he said, "He that

believeth on me, the works that I do shall he do also and greater works than these shall he do." Those who take up the Cross and go forward are able to do astonishing things. The Mennonites, who were driven out of Russia, are putting into practice a wholly cooperative enterprise in Brazil.* Nominal communism is worthless, but the communism of this group springs out of Christ's teaching. We have determined to take up the Cross and go forward, each in the sphere revealed to him. Let us guard against falling into sentimentalism, or against being carried away by this or that new tendency of the times. We are apt to fall into such errors. We must press on, carrying the Cross, each with a clear understanding of our individual mission in life. Before throwing the dice we must make sure whether it is heads or tails we mean to choose. I say of myself that I must be a gambler for God. Fully awake to this redemptive purpose of God, and consciously sharing in his love, I must heal this stricken corner of the world. When Japan has grown better, some of us will have to pour out our energies for China. The civilization of the world had its origin in China.

In whatever place we are, whether in some remote village far up in the mountains, or as a school-teacher in some tiny township on the plain, we must bestir ourselves and take up our Cross in that very place. If we face with aversion the office-ledgers we have to keep, we must realize that here lies the Cross for us. Only by patiently writing one ideograph after another is the manuscript ever completed. Let us advance, then, with our hearts filled with this consciousness of the Cross. Freed from every sort of error in our conceptions, let us press on, in

* The Mennonites, driven out of Russia, went both to Brazil and Paraguay, but their success has been more conspicuous and their numbers larger in the latter country.

philosophy, in science, and in theology, and most of all in our realization of the Cross.

PRAYER

O God our Father: Show to each of us the Cross which he must bear. Even though it be a path of suffering which stretches before us, help us to press on, fully conscious of the Cross, even to that final moment when we draw our last breath. Do not let us become too accustomed to peaceful paths and easy level roads, but give us the consciousness of the Cross, and teach us to share in the redemptive purpose of God, that we may make Japan into the Kingdom of God. We pray this in Jesus' name. Amen.

XII

DIVINE LOVE MADE REAL THROUGH
THE CROSS

*Beloved, let us love one another: for love is of God;
and every one that loveth is begotten of God, and
knoweth God. He that loveth not knoweth not God;
for God is love.* I John 4:7, 8.

"THE GREEKS gave us learning, the Romans law, but
what has Christ given us?" asks the Polish novelist Sien-
kiewicz in his novel *Quo Vadis*. He goes on to answer the
question by declaring that Christ has given love to the
world. And the love which Christ taught was not merely
an affection towards those to whom one is naturally attracted. In Japan we think of love simply as attraction
toward those we like. I often hear people say they know
what it is to love, without the help of Christian teaching.
But Christ taught us to love those whom we dislike. Men
think this supremely difficult. The lofty love of the weak,
the poverty-stricken, the crippled, is the actual practice of
the gospel. Though it is impossible to love these folk by
merely human effort, we can do so by the power of God.

"Nonsense!" someone will say scornfully. "If one
dislikes another, he dislikes him, and that's that!" Such
folks talk about incompatibility. If a husband and wife
quarrel constantly, the husband says, "She irritates me.
I can't help it. It's my nature; I was born that way."
And the wife says, "With my temperament I cannot put
up with a man like that!" It is just that temperament

we are born with, however, which must be made over again. If we have been changed and caused to grow, we must make every effort to love others. This is the effort of life. Some will say it is unreasonable to expect it. Is it really possible? If not, then the nineteen-hundred-years-old gospel of Christ is a falsehood.

Though it lasted but three years, the activity of Jesus changed the course of history. We can trace its influence down through these nineteen hundred years to the present. What, then, did Jesus do during these three years? He taught, he was active in doing good, and he was conscious of his mission. We can understand his activity, but unless we have come under the sway of his influence, we cannot understand this consciousness.

Tolstoy had a tremendous admiration for Jesus; he regarded him as one of the prophets, and declared that if the Sermon on the Mount alone had been preserved, it would have been quite enough. Tolstoy had no interest in religion till he was past fifty years of age. He won world-wide fame by his novel, *Anna Karenina,* but he confessed that he had committed every sort of crime that man could commit. He had broken every one of the Ten Commandments. He had committed murder, adultery, he had lied, he had gambled, he had neglected his parents, he had not worshipped God. Needless to say he had broken the Sabbath and profaned the name of God before others. He had been an idolater, joining in the cult of the worship of Self. But while he was thus breaking the Ten Commandments, he had become famous, and he thought himself a most extraordinary man. At fifty years of age his soul began to awake, and his heart to throb with pain. There was one thing, so he discovered, that he had never yet done, and that was to love. In despair and disgust with his life, he tried again and again to put an end to himself by taking a pistol and shooting himself, but somehow he could never bring himself to pull the trigger. He resolved to do that one thing that he had never done — to love. And so he came back to Christ's teaching in the Sermon on the Mount, to love others as one's self.

It was because of this experience that Tolstoy revered the Sermon on the Mount above all other teaching. But had Christ only taught, without putting his teaching into practice, I doubt if I should admire him. It is a splendid thing, of course, to have the Sermon on the Mount, but even without that record of Christ's teaching, Christ's priceless experience upon the Cross would bring home to me, with tremendous force, the love of God.

THE SEVEN WORDS FROM THE CROSS

Christ spoke seven Words on the Cross. In a previous chapter I have treated them from the point of view of his consciousness, but here I want to discuss them in the light of the Social Movement. First, he said, since those who have put me on the Cross did it without understanding what it was all about, please forgive them. Second, to the robber he said, " Today thou shalt be with me in Paradise." Third, he took care of his mother. Fourth, he sang the first line of the twenty-second psalm, " My God, My God, why hast Thou forsaken me? " Fifth, he said, " I thirst." Sixth, he cried, " It is finished." Seventh, " Father, into Thy hands I commend my spirit." Praying thus he departed from this world. The more I think of these seven Words the more I seem to learn from them greater things than even from the long discourse of the Sermon on the Mount.

In the first place, Christ had the experience of loving his enemies. At the very moment when Christ was hanging upon the Cross, he loved, not only those to whom he was bound by ties of affection, but also those for whom he had a natural aversion. When we use the word "love" here in Japan, we immediately think of love between the sexes, and we do not count as love, love which is felt towards those who hang one on a Cross. This love is something immensely difficult to practice. Although among the famous men of Japanese history there are not a few of superior character, there are none who showed any love for those who subjected them to death. In our famous ghost stories we find a spirit of revenge. The victim is pictured as taking vengeance in every possible way upon the one who has injured him. Even Sakura Sogoro shows this same spirit, and a flood of resentment surged through him as he felt death approaching. But Christ, who felt as God feels, forgave his enemies for crucifying him.

When we hear this story of Christ's forgiveness, our hearts are stirred, and we wish that we, too, could forgive as he did. But when someone even steps on our toes in a streetcar, how do we act? We feel like giving him a piece of our mind and we grumble and say, "What's the matter with you, anyhow? Can't you be a bit careful?" Our practice is not in line with our wishful thinking. But Christ, who shared the heart of God, was able to say without a shadow of constraint, and with absolute serenity of spirit, "Father, forgive them, for they do not know what they are doing."

It is this spirit which has flowed down through the years from Christ's heart and has entered deeply into the hearts of those who long to know him, and to be like him. Through the power of this spirit this dark world becomes a world of light. Christ did not come to make good men into good men, but his purpose was to lift very wicked men into the status of children of God. This is out of the range of possibility from the standpoint of human accomplishment. Unless one has entered deeply into a conscious sharing of God's spirit, such love towards men does not spring up in one's heart.

It is indisputable that Christ loved his enemies, for he possessed the love and power of God. Humanly speaking, it is impossible to love one's enemies, and to talk in friendly fashion with a prostitute; but Christ walked the road together with a woman who was living in adultery. He took a meal with a collector of taxes, and he lived with a man, one of his own disciples, who was so radical as to be opposed to paying taxes. He loved children, though in that day they were chattels, and among his comrades were women, though the position of women in society in those days was very low. He drew to himself and loved the most worthless among the sick, the lepers, the unemployed, and the despairing. It is a tremendously difficult thing to care for and support helpless women and children and those whom the world counts as insignificant. Today in the farming villages we often find those who feel that women are impure and unclean, and therefore unfit to share in the worship of the gods. These village people, too, are outspoken in their abhorrence of lepers, and of women who fall into adultery.

I once paid a call on the Vice-Minister of Parliamentary Affairs at the Department of Justice. When I asked this man to give some work to the unemployed, he said to me, " Kagawa San, do you realize that the most pitiable men in Japan are the ex-convicts? "* How are these men

* But the government is doing something to remedy matters. Just as this chapter is being read, comes from Japan the issue of the Japan Advertiser, an English newspaper published by Americans, for September 1, 1935, in which appears the following headline:

PRISON WINS PRAISE OF U. S. SOCIOLOGIST

Visitor to Fuchu Prison (Tokyo) Impressed by Rarity of Escapes
Despite Easy Opportunities

Cleanliness is Lauded

treated, as a general thing? If a man is once sentenced and sent to prison, he is dubbed a jail-bird by the world, even though he may have been committed for such a slight offence as stealing a piece of fish. At one time in the slum in which I lived there was a sort of epidemic of baby-killing, that is, of allowing foster-children who had been placed in the homes to die of neglect. That year of 1911 there were fourteen funerals of such foster-children, and in 1912 there were nineteen, for times were hard those years. That year a woman living in my home, the wife of

---

Inmates' Spirit of Atonement Contrasted with Attitude of American Convicts

One mind seems to be at work in a Japanese prison; in an American prison two minds are at work in diametrically opposed directions. That, according to Dr. Jesse Steiner, head of the department of sociology of the University of Washington, appears, from first impressions, to be the distinction between a Japanese and an American prison. "What impressed me first were the comparatively low and thin walls that surround the prison, which would please American prisoners intent upon escape. I was next impressed, when I entered the prison, with the utter lack of odors found in most prisons. The Fuchu prison is also a fine example of cleanliness and appears more like a modern apartment house than a prison. I found the disgusting prison atmosphere lacking. Compared with the numerous escapes in the United States the Fuchu prison record of two escapes in four years is understandable, for the conditions obtaining there represent kindly treatment of all inmates. Particularly noticeable was the way in which the cells are laid out. Unlike the thick, strong double bars employed in American prisons, those of the Fuchu prison are small. From the American point of view, cells with such bars would permit easy escape. The system of outside cell construction is employed in the Fuchu prison, one side of the cell opening to the corridor and the other facing the outside, allowing the sunlight to enter. An inmate could escape, if he wanted to, by sawing the bars of his window. The inside cell construction method is generally used in American prisons, and the prisoner who is intent on escape would have to saw the bars of his cell and then the bars of the window, if any, on the outside.

"Food in the Fuchu prison appeared very nourishing, though it was simple. Strict discipline and good order seemed to be observed by the 2,300 inmates there. . . . What I observed in the Fuchu prison seemed to show that the policy in Japan is educative and not punitive. Through strict discipline, favorable living conditions, work and educational lectures,

a pirate of the Inland Sea, stole a garment worth sixteen sen and was sentenced to six months' imprisonment, at hard labor. I know what difficulties these ex-convicts meet in trying to make a living.

Christ loved even those who, like the ex-convicts of today, were pointed at with the finger of scorn. He did not keep his distance from these men, but mingled with them without the least hesitation. If I should walk along the street with a geisha, I would certainly be criticized for it. Christ was looked down upon for mixing with such folk.

A woman with her hair hanging in loose disorder around her face anointed the feet of Christ with nard and wiped them with her hair. The Pharisees were indig-

---

every opportunity is afforded the inmates to atone for their crimes and leave the prison better men.

"American criminals enter prisons with the idea of serving time and of getting out as soon as they possibly can. Japanese criminals are apparently in prison to atone for their crimes, for it seemed to me that the spirit of atonement was quietly alive. The administration apparently trusts that spirit, which seems to augment the comparatively weak construction of the cells. . . ."

This reminds us of the 1923 earthquake in Tokyo, when the entire population of a certain prison in Tokyo especially for those condemned to life imprisonment might have escaped through the fallen walls. Not a man fled. The prison warden marshalled them like a regiment of soldiers, directed them how to leave the ruined buildings, and found them absolutely under discipline though in the open for hours practically without guards. They were as loyal as the guards themselves.

There are in Japan a number of refuges for ex-convicts conducted by Christians. Some will remember the work of the late Caroline Macdonald, who wrote A Gentleman in Prison, from the lifestory of a condemned man as written by himself soon after his conversion and shortly before his execution. Miss Macdonald had many stories of released ex-convicts who are living a life of usefulness and have lived down the social ostracism which is customary.

All this bears on Kagawa's emphasis on atonement and social solidarity, suggesting him to be a product as well as a molder of his social process. — H. T.

nant. " What's this? " they grumbled. " Do you know
what sort of life this woman has led? " Jesus did not re-
buke them by saying, " See here, don't insult her! " but
he began to tell a story exactly to the point. " Simon,"
said he, " if a man who had borrowed five hundred yen
and one who had borrowed fifty yen both had their debts
forgiven, which of the two would be the happier? This
woman was in debt to God and that debt had just now
been forgiven."

There is a story in the Gospel of John which tells how
Christ dealt with a woman caught in the act of adultery,
and helped her. The Pharisees had dragged her into the
presence of Christ. " Hey there," they cried, " you Jesus,
look at this hussy! She's been caught in the very act of
adultery. Shall we stone her to death? Or what shall we
do with her? " Christ made no reply, but leaned over
and drew pictures in the sand. " See here! Aren't you
going to answer us? " To this Christ replied, " If there
is one of you who has nothing in the least to be ashamed
of, let him throw the first stone at the woman." " What's
that? " " Anyone who has nothing on his conscience —
just wait a moment. . . . Say, you throw it. I don't feel
just like it." So each one tried to pass the responsibility
to his fellow; then one by one they began to leave the
place till none but Christ and the woman remained.
"Woman," said he, " Is there no one to accuse you? "
" No, no one." " Then neither do I judge you."

Christ spoke again exactly to the point. If he had been
a novelist he would have asked the woman where and how
and all about it, but Christ was not a novelist. He understood how the woman felt. Christ's sympathies were
many-sided. He was not a stickler for the letter of the
law. Neither was he swayed unduly by his sympathy
for the woman. Christ always dared to press forward

with intrepid courage to God's viewpoint, and to feel as God feels. His attitude fills me with the deepest admiration.

THE HISTORICAL DEVELOPMENT OF DIVINE LOVE

St. Paul made his appearance in the first century, and in the second century we find such men as Origen, a philosopher of Egypt, writing books on Christian doctrine. But it is more interesting still to see the early Christians putting into practice the principles of divine love. When an epidemic of the plague broke out during the second century, and thousands were dying, the Christians, who had been suffering all sorts of ill-treatment, organized into a group called *Paralobani,* and went about taking care of the very people who had been dragging them off to prison. Later they formed a sort of cooperative society for burying the dead, a task which no one else was willing to undertake. These early Christians, however, quite willingly undertook to serve the needs of the sick, and to bury the dead. The story of their loving service moves me to tears whenever I read it.

There are many stories of early Christians who gave themselves in some such way. I have already told you of Gallicanus who founded the first hospital. I am amazed when I read of his activities. In the third century the practice of Christian love spread all over Europe. In the fourth century the first refuge for lepers in the world was established in the city of Antioch in Asia Minor. In the year 370 A.D. St. Basil, a leader in the church, began to help the unemployed. It was the custom in those cruel days for the fund for the unemployed to be used to hire men to fight each other to the death in the arena. A man called Telemachus leaped down into the arena in protest against the custom. He lost his life, but as a consequence of his act, this cruel and wicked custom ceased to be practiced.

One after another, all kinds of movements expressing Christian love sprang up. In France the young Christian community was taught works of love by its founder, Martin. Ireland was instructed in such enterprises by Patrick; Slovakia by Ulfilas. Christianity penetrated Europe through and through. It was not merely a philosophy; had it been merely that, it would not have gone so deep. Martin, for instance, had a great deal of sympathy with the serfs in their tenancy disputes. When he was told how the landowners were ill-treating their tenants, he came to the tenants' help. To this day Martin, though a native of Jugoslavia, who devoted his life to preaching the gospel in France, is revered there as the guardian and patron saint of the French villages.

The way in which Europe was led to Christ was quite different from the way Christianity came into Japan. It was through the practice of love rather than through philosophy. In those dark days of the Middle Ages one could have seen black-masked figures passing to and fro along the streets of the towns of Italy. They were not burglars, but nurses of the sick, who wore these masks so that they might not be recognized by others. Silently they went about on their errands of mercy, tending the sick, and then as quietly returned to their homes. One finds the Cross on many of the European national flags. The intention seems to be to commemorate those early European Christians who died through persecution.

We all know the story of the Crusades. Sometimes we Orientals are inclined to remember only the blood-thirsty men of Europe. But we must not forget also that there were many brave and yet chivalrous knights who did not oppress the weak but were filled with the spirit of Christ.

They served the needs of the weak and poverty-stricken. This spirit of chivalry had an historic influence upon Bushido, the Way of the Knight, in Japan. The Catholic fathers brought chivalry to our country. Before their coming the old records show that in the olden days in Japan men's heads had been exchanged even for the silver trappings on the heads of the harness, but with the entrance of Christianity into Japan things changed. The martyrdom of the Catholic Christians of that day introduced a new element into Japanese experience.

We have already referred to Yukinaga Konishi who was crucified in the capital for the sake of his principles. Such sacrifices instilled a new spirit in Japan. A spirit of loyalty was developed in marked contrast to that of the older days when every man had his price. They learned to love to the uttermost, and to die for their faith. The Japanese creed of loyalty, that is the spirit of Bushido, is permeated with the spirit of Christianity.

In Europe St. Francis and Saint Louis were outstanding exemplars of the love of the cross. Again in the fourteenth century we find Wycliffe; in the fifteenth, Savonarola; in the sixteenth, the Anabaptists, who carried on a sort of communism. Later came the Moravian brotherhood and in the eighteenth century the movement of John Wesley. All through the ages, though the ruling classes gave themselves up to slaughtering one another, among the laborers and the lower strata of society movements of mutual love and helpfulness continued to grow. In the nineteenth century also, there were men who, like Livingstone and George Williams, practiced love in the places where they preached the Way. In Japan, also, Christianity will be no longer of value if we eliminate Christ's teaching of love, the practice of love, and the consciousness of love — that is, the practice of the love of the Cross. The only way to reconstruct our society is to make Christ's teaching, " Love one another," real and actual, here and now.

When I think of these movements started by the disciples of Christ in Europe I ask, have we in Japan the courage to press forward on the road of the Cross? Or have we not? It is not real Christianity merely to carry a gilt-edged Bible and hymn book to church on Sunday, like an upper-class person. Individual worship of God is not enough. The church must be transformed into a mutual aid organization, a society for the realization of Love-in-action. Shall we not actually start movements among ourselves for the practical expression of love? Having begun them, not one of us should back out. It was by such activities that Europe was transformed.

To tell the truth, love is dangerous. It is a " dangerous thought " for a money lender to talk about lending money without interest; and the ideal of monogamy, with husband and wife true to each other, is too narrow a doctrine to suit the house of ill-fame. It is quite possible that the very sincerity of our love may be misunderstood, and we may be put to death. If you are afraid of that you had better not start out on this venture.

Let us advance on this enterprise of love with sober hearts. Then a new reverence for life, a new respect for labor, will spring up in our hearts. Until Christ came, labor was considered the lot of slaves. In Japan, too, the laborer used to be little better than a slave. But when we learned from Christ that God himself is a laborer (John 5:17) it revolutionized our attitude towards labor in Japan. Materialism makes man into a machine, into a commodity, into something that can be exchanged for money. But human beings are neither machines nor commodities, nor are they in the same class with money. We are personalities.

No one but Christ has ever taught reverence for personality. One social theory after another comes into prominence, but unless they are founded on Christ they do not have any real reverence for personality. Russia has advocated an industrialized nation, but if this ideal is not rooted in the idea of personality, she will go astray. Productive industry has come into being for the sake of mankind, not mankind for the sake of industry.

The only way to establish the Kingdom of God on earth is by Love movements. Stokes of India, though an outstanding missionary, left his work in the city and went barefoot into the villages where pestilence was rife. At first, the villagers ridiculed him, giving him rotten fruit to eat from a cracked bowl. But he sought out the most despised person in the village and loved him. Because of this work of love in their midst, those who had abhorred Christianity gradually came to admire Stokes. In the end they reverenced him and gave him the title of Maharajah, that is, Great Prince.

A REAL CHRISTIANITY

How did it come about that Christianity spread throughout Japan in the Meiji period? Perhaps it was partly because people read books and read the Bible. But this was far from being the sole reason. It was because such men as Niijima, Paul Sawayama, Juji Ishii, and others, bore the Cross, and thus showed Christ to the people of Japan. Not only such as these; Christianity exists today in Japan because there were many saints who bore the Cross in unseen places. There was Sadajiro Hongo, who abandoned the life of an official in order to live the life of a beggar. There was Nobue Terajima, who founded an old people's home, while earning her living as a nurse. There was Junbei Homma, a carpenter who by his own efforts founded a reformatory. There was Mrs. Kieko Yamamuro, who though she had an unusual education, forsook her cultured home to live a life of sacrifice; and Keiko Hattori, a woman who offered her short life for the sake of lepers. There was a host of lesser saints who took up the Cross, unknown to the world at large. Because of such as these, the movement of love realized in practice in remote villages and out-of-the-way places, has borne fruit throughout Japan.

I pray that we may each in his own sphere — the teacher in the school, the nurse in the hospital — actualize the spirit of Christ by helping those in greater need than ourselves. Then the Kingdom of God will be established in Japan. We must make real and actual the love of God, the God of heaven and earth. If we pray, it can be done. It becomes possible only when we first resolve to follow the Cross. All the various reconstruction movements — the Consumers' Cooperative movement, the Workers' Education movement, the Labor movement, and the one for increasing production — must be founded upon the love of the Cross. Some will go to the fishing villages, others to the farming regions. Each will feel his own special mission. Let each of us grasp the consciousness of the Cross, and reveal all we can of Christ.

Moreover, love movements cannot be undertaken separately in an individualistic scattered fashion. We must band ourselves together. Names make no difference whatever. Let all of us who love Christ gather together under one banner.

In the Meiji period, people became Christians at the risk of their lives. But today we often find homes where, though the parents are Christian, the children have drifted away from the faith. Is it possible that the Christians of today are cowardly? There are many things I would like to say to those homes, and I would like to speak plainly. I challenge you all to bestir yourselves. Gather under the banner of Christ!

PRAYER

O Father of Purity: We confess that Japan, this land of ours, is this very day shut up in darkness; voices of lamentation rise on every hand, from the farming villages and from the fishing villages which are in distress. We beseech Thee to have pity upon the hundreds of unemployed who wander to and fro on the streets of our cities! O take possession of the hearts of our youth in this day of trouble! Teach them plainly that Japan is to be saved through the Way of the Cross and through Love, and not by force, not by military power. Though the road, the Way of the Cross, which we must follow, is not a pleasant nor an easy path, strengthen us in our resolution to walk this road! Do Thou be our Shield, and help us. May Thy Kingdom draw near throughout Japan, in the villages, the mines, the factories, the schoolrooms, the offices. Comfort those who lie sick with pestilence in the pest-hospitals; those who lie helpless in tuberculosis hospitals; those who live in homes for lepers. We will press forward with boldness on Thy path; therefore, O God, make us Thy messengers, and grant that new movements, new enterprises of love may spring up among us. This we pray through our Savior Jesus Christ. Amen.

XIII

LOVING GOD IN SOCIETY

*But emptied himself, taking the form of a servant,
being made in the likeness of man.* Philippians 2:7.

THERE was a remarkable development of Christianity in
Japan during the reign of the Meiji Emperor, from 1868
to 1912. This Meiji Era was the first after the abolition
of feudalism, while the social classes were struggling pain-
fully upwards. Many individuals experienced suffering
and therefore easily grasped the idea of redemption. The
Christians of that day accepted the need of salvation but
were not yet thoroughly grounded in its theoretical basis.
Accordingly when the new theology came into Japan,
about the middle of the Meiji period, salvation from sin
and the idea of redemptive love were gradually rejected.
Even in the Christian churches there were many who
did not believe in redemption from sin. Probably there
are people among us today who do not consider it necessary to think much about this, even though they do appreciate the self-giving sacrifice of Jesus.

We shall never understand redemption merely with the
intellect. The New Testament writers were not perform-
ing a merely intellectual task. It was not physics or other
natural sciences which produced the sacred canon. It was
the deep, suffering experience of the human soul which,
written down, became the scripture records.

When the famous twelfth century Buddhist priest,

Honen Shonin, preached his doctrine of " salvation by the help of another," his first converts were two concubines of the retired Emperor Shirakawa. As a result Honen was banished for eight years. In modern times we have a similar example of a certain Yokotaro Nakagawa, of Okayama province, who thought it would be a good thing to import Western culture and incidentally Christianity. The first person to accept this new faith was his own concubine, Koume Sumiya, from the depths of her misery. When Nakagawa heard that she had become a believer in Christianity, he ceased to support her. (And also closed the preaching place.) But she turned out to be a regular Mary Magdalene. She went to Kobe College and studied, and then for forty years pressed forward earnestly in the way of Christ, leading many other women to enter into the same experience, among whom was at least one of the highest social position, one Rosho Toyotake. Koume took as her life-motto the words, " No other crown but the Cross." She was highly respected and known as the " Woman Sage of Okayama Prefecture." In the novel, *A Japanese,* which I read a while ago, one of the characters is styled " a saintly concubine." At first I thought the author had imagined the character, but learned later that he had merely depicted this Koume Sumiya.

One of her contemporaries in the Okayama Christian community was a medical student. Through taking care of a pilgrim, a poor woman with two children, he had a deep spiritual experience and devoted his life thereafter to charity work. This was none other than the famous Juji Ishii, the first man to establish an orphanage in Japan. But Ishii was very much helped by Koume. When he was hard put to it to feed the many children in his orphanage, he used always to go up the mountain to pray. It

was Koume who would then immediately start out to col-
lect funds for Ishii.   On my visits to Okayama prefecture
today I find a comparatively large number of Christians in
its towns and rural districts, and most of them have been
influenced directly or indirectly toward the Christian
faith by these two personalities.   Thereby the possibilities
of the actual practice of love have been impressed afresh
upon me.   Theoretical discussions of " social science "
have their fervent advocates, who forget to redeem the
individual from sin; but I cannot help but ponder upon
how many people Koume, the redeemed concubine, was
able to bring under the influence of Christ!

THE AWAKENING OF CONSCIENCE AND THE SENSE OF SOCIAL SOLIDARITY

I am conscious of the religion of atoning love.   The
gospel of Jesus is easily grasped by him who knows his
sin.   But when as in this materialistic present even the
killing of another human being is not thought of as sin,
Christ is hard to understand.   We admit that it is wrong
to kill an individual but we do not think it wrong to kill in
war.   That is, as individuals we are conscious, but we are
not yet fully conscious of the Whole.   We do not have the
consciousness that Christ possessed of the God of heaven
and earth, and the sober thought of seeking forgiveness.
In this present age of machine civilization, man also is a
machine.   He declines all responsibility.*

There are three stages in the development of consciousness — unconsciousness, semi-consciousness and full consciousness.   From unconsciousness to semi-conscious
awakening, and then onward to full consciousness — the
Scriptures record the development of the human race, and
it is a long story.   The Scriptures are a laboratory, a re-

* For this use of the word " responsibility," cf. footnote on p. 64.

search field, for mankind. Here is the tale of man's failures and rebellions, all the way from the Garden of Eden
down to the Roman Era, and of God's desire to save him,
crystallized into a written record. Since at first man was
unconscious, there was a shameful age, that of the Judges.
In that dark day, since it was necessary to give men consciousness of sin, that they might have forgiveness, and
since it would not do to kill human beings, it became the
thing to do to offer a lamb by way of apology to God.
That is the atonement. Although there are among us
those who say, " That was superstition! What possible
effect could the killing of a lamb have? " The custom
arose from a real and deep need of the soul.

In looking up the history of Greek morals I have read
Development of Greek Religion by Fannel, an expert on
Greek civilization, and have learned that until the ninth
century B.C. even in that wonderful civilization of Greece
it was not thought wrong to commit murder. But when
conscience awakened, the more it was aroused the more
necessary became salvation. The longing emerged to
wash away the blood of the person who had been slain.
The Greeks believed in a religion of nature and worshipped the sun. Later they acquired Persian religion,
and would go to the mountains and make confession of
their sins all night long. This gradually became a religion
of conversion, the religion of Dionysius. And from that
stage they came at last to believe in Christ alone. " The
time was fulfilled " as Mark has it in 1:15. By the second
century B.C. the Greek Gnostics were teaching a conscience religion and the need of a savior.

In Old Testament times the people received atonement
through the blood of a lamb, but as they passed from semi-
consciousness to consciousness, they came to feel that " I

as a human being must offer up my own blood; " (that is, redemption-consciousness). "And not for my own sins alone, for the sins of others have some connection with my own faults " — this because one's own consciousness has become fully awakened. Christ's dying as a substitute for many sinners is, like the backing of a promissory note, an expression of the sense of social solidarity. Without a consciousness of responsibility for the sins of others, we can never have a sense of social solidarity.

The sense of joint responsibility penetrates the consciousness of those who have any experience of paying for the blunders of others, but even these forget the people with whom they are not immediately concerned. But Jesus had practically attained to the full consciousness of God, and thought of his responsibility toward Chinese, Koreans and even Japanese without discrimination — all are sons of Abraham! And if we follow this thought through, our eyes will be opened to the fact that we have responsibility for even the most depraved, the geisha, or women of the licensed quarters. It is when we awaken to this fact that we truly believe in God. Those who have not yet had their eyes opened to this consciousness of the Whole are not yet awake to social solidarity.

There are nine thousand or more delinquents annually in the city of Tokyo. Who is responsible for these nine thousand young people? How many are there who are conscious of any responsibility for their sins? Those who feel no concern have not yet understood the Cross. Those who have come into a full consciousness are atonement-conscious. To set about to redeem these delinquents is to share consciously in the atonement. I must become as awake as God himself to my responsibility for all living creatures in the universe, and realize the fact that I have a relation to them all. We cannot comprehend this with our modern theology. This atonement-consciousness was very clear in Masahisa Uemura.*

From my experience of living among the poor, I am opposed to the idea that it is enough to change their outward environment, or to distribute material goods or cash among them. The economic aspect is only one phase of human activity, and we can never reorganize society from that standpoint alone. The faults of men must be swept away. Social reconstruction is impossible without seeking first a deep spiritual awakening.

THE UNITY OF THE RELIGION OF CONSCIENCE AND THE SOCIAL MOVEMENT

In Russia today they deny the validity of all religion, especially of the Christian religion. They are not succeeding that way. Nor do we know of any successful attempt anywhere to disregard the thousands of years of the history of conscience. The development of conscience and of the social movement must go on together.

In a selfish movement Christ's teachings are meaningless. It is not enough to surrender our sins to Christ; we must shoulder responsibility for others. It is at this point that conscience-religion and the social movement become one and the same.

The Japan of today which in former days drifted into the currents of modernism, will probably be more and more wrought up over the problem of sex. Unless Japan can have a pure attitude toward sex, like that of God, she will perish.

When the festival celebrating the ascension to the throne of the present Emperor was held in 1928, for fear of some untoward incident the police interned about sixty-

* A famous Japanese Christian minister of a former generation.

nine thousand insane persons, but that was only part of our insane population. According to a survey made of eighty-six villages by the Department of Public Health of the Home Office, nineteen out of every thousand persons are suffering from mental diseases. If this proportion holds true of the whole of Japan, there must be some one hundred and twenty thousand insane in the whole country. According to Dr. Kure, twenty-five out of every thousand are insane. This would give us at least one hundred and fifty thousand mental patients in this country. If this is true, insanity is increasing at the rate of six per cent per year. The chief causes of mental diseases, especially of the type which results in palsy and in mental weakness, are syphilis and alcoholism.

Suppose an era of communism should come! A communism which means merely a communism in the production of material things is not a real communism. Unless people come to think of the sins of others as their own sin, it is impossible to bring about real social reconstruction. Without the desire for a clean conscience there can be no social movement. It takes three men to carry on communist propaganda — one carries a pistol, one a dagger, and one pastes bills. It is said that communists have killed policemen in Osaka, Kobe and Wakayama. How can we be indifferent in the face of such atrocities?

In their violence, the communists utterly disregard conscience. At the beginning of the Russian movement, such men as Bakunin did carry on enterprises which expressed love for humanity, but later they ceased that sort of activity, and instead they formed secret societies and fell to making plots which in the end cost them their lives. Germany suffers one disorder after another until she is changed into an inferno before our very eyes. Therein we also share responsibility.

When we commit ourselves wholly to our love for society, and join the ranks of the lower classes, we must always keep a clear consciousness of atoning love. To share in the redemptive purpose of atoning love and in the movement for social reconstruction, we must have the Christ-consciousness. We find it explained in the Scriptures in various ways that God did not create man and cause him to develop a physiological body, only to cast him aside for time and eternity as morally worthless. When we meditate on this truth in relation to our own souls, we realize the significance of Christ, the One who died on the Cross, and the realization of this profound truth brings us into a personal and intimate relationship with him. The ninth chapter of Hebrews records the history of the consciousness of atonement, from earliest times, when civilization was unknown. The New Testament, with its full-orbed consciousness of God, reveals God's intention to carry the debts of mankind himself. Even when men fail, God accepts this as his own failure. This is the overflowing grace of God. Whenever I think of it, it fills my heart with joy.

THE LIFE OF AN ACROBAT

It is now almost twenty-four years since I received baptism. It was in a Christian preaching-place in Tokushima, where among the group of Christians there was at that time a lame man by the name of Hosokawa. His father had been a doctor in Osaka. When Hosokawa was in the third year of middle school, he went to the bad, left home, and went up to Tokyo. There he became a tight-rope walker and acrobat. As such he crossed the ocean to America, travelled about England, and Germany, and Austria. One day, when he was about to give a performance in the city of Vienna, he did not feel as well as usual and in the midst of a wonderful feat of tight-rope walking, in which he prided himself, he fell from the rope. As luck would have it, the net beneath had not been securely strung that day, with the result that he struck his backbone, and was seriously injured.

For a long time he lay in the Roman Catholic hospital in Vienna, but made no recovery. At last, when he had become completely paralyzed, he was sent back to his home in Kobe, with his passage paid. On arriving in Japan, he felt too much ashamed to go to his father. He could not walk; what was he to do? In his abject misery, he began to beg. He could crawl along for a distance of one or two blocks in an hour. He thought that if he could only visit the famous image of Kobo Daishi at Tatsue in the island of Shikoku, he might be cured. With this hope, he crossed the straits over to the city of Tokushima in Shikoku. Day after day he kept on crawling along in the direction of the famous image. But when at last he arrived there, he was disappointed. The Buddhist priest beat him and threw him out.

He was beaten but not defeated. "All right," he said to himself, "I will go and ask help at the Christian church. I can never forget the kindness shown me in the hospital at Vienna. There must be a kind Christian church somewhere in Japan, too. I will go and find it myself." So he started out and after a journey of three or four days, he came to Tokushima, and Dr. Logan helped him. After awhile he began to recover and was able to stand on his feet. He began to go about the streets with a little cart, selling cooked sweet potatoes. For nine years he lived the life of faith, with his heart filled with joy, until finally he died as a result of his former injuries.

This man's story taught me a deep lesson. Life here on this earth is like this man's career. We are continually having to meet the hard blows of life, and we go about in a futile search for help, for salvation, but there is no salvation except in Christ. When I saw this man and heard his story, I determined not to travel the road of life which he had followed, but from the outset to travel the road of the Cross.

Some say that they have no faults, that they have never failed; but it is only Christ who has attained perfection. And it was he, the Sinless One, who bore the sins of men and travelled the road of the Cross. We, too, must take this way of the Cross. We must live in redeeming love. Therein lies the synthesis between redeeming love and the love of society.

PRAYER

Heavenly Father: Teach us of the privileged classes, whose lives are filled with every blessing, to take a step forward into the road of redemptive love. Although Jesus himself was without sin, he took the faults of men upon himself, and carried the Cross of redemptive love. We have not sincerely undertaken the life of faith. We idle our days away in listlessness. We are unconscious or only half-conscious of life's challenge. Awaken us, O God, that we may with sincerity carry the burdens of others. Grant that we may not be content to live empty lives, seeking only the pleasure that each day brings. Cause us to advance to the Cross. All society lies under a shadow, and we are apprehensive over the future of Japan. Our consciences are clouded. Awake us, O God, to our responsibility for sufferers in the depths of misery. Inspire us to undertake to save them, in the Spirit of Jesus, till at length all mankind will join in singing praises to Thy name. And this I pray in the name of our Lord Jesus. Amen.

XIV

THE CROSS AND SOCIAL LIFE

This is my commandment, that ye love one another,
even as I have loved you. Greater love hath no man
than this, that a man lay down his life for his friends.
John 15:12, 13.

WHY was it that Jesus had to choose the Cross? Let us reflect on this point.

There are some Western scholars who declare that there are two systems of Christianity, the Pauline system of thought and the Christ system of thought. I do not agree with this view. Christ could not definitely declare himself to be the Christ until he had hung upon the Cross. There was something which he, as long as he was alive, could not explain to others. When Peter confessed to his belief and said, " Thou art the Christ," Jesus did not say, " Yes, that is so." He told Peter that his confession was inspired by God but to keep silent about it. And then he went on to say that in a short time he himself would be crucified. Why did Jesus thus over and over again talk in such an incomprehensible way?

When John the Baptist sent his messengers from prison, to ask, " Art thou the Messiah? " Jesus replied, " The blind receive their sight, and the lame walk, the lepers are cleansed, and the deaf hear, the dead are raised to life and the poor have good tidings preached to them." Why could he not say, " Yes, it is true, I am " ?

There are two mountain peaks in Christ's path to the Cross: one, when John was put into prison, and the second, the death of John. Christ began his work immediately after John had been put into prison. It was then that John questioned him. Christ replied, " Look at the facts, see what is happening." But he did not plainly assert his claims. The true Christ would certainly be a Christ who suffered on the Cross. He could not rest assured of his Messiahship until he had fulfilled the prophecies of the Twenty-Second Psalm and the fifty-third chapter of Isaiah. He could not command men to worship him. Jesus realized that he would become the Christ only when he had completely offered up his life. It was because of this conviction that he commanded Peter, at the time of his confession, to guard the secret, for he had not yet brought his work to completion through suffering death.

The second crisis occurred when John was given the death penalty. His disciples, as soon as they had buried him in Samaria, came in all haste to Christ. There were about five thousand of them, and this revolutionary crowd wanted to put Jesus forward as their leader. Strauss makes the assertion that the story here contains material which has been invented, based on the traditions handed down about Elijah, which is here clumsily interjected into the record. But in the fifteenth verse of the sixth chapter of John it is recorded that the crowd was about to take him by force and make him king. The gospels of Matthew, Mark and Luke were written earlier, and it is quite certain that they deleted all reference to this incident which bordered on insurrection, because it would have been dangerous at that time to record it, as it would have brought them into suspicion from the administrative officials. But the Gospel of John was written in Patmos; John wrote without the least fear of administrative offi-

cials. He went on to write the Revelation in the same
unstudied style. Although persecution was at its height,
he was utterly fearless and wrote without reserve or
anxiety as to the outcome.

Christ said, " If you do not eat my flesh and drink my
blood, there can be no true spiritual revolution." He declared that it was not sufficient to be concerned with the
problems of the Mosaic law, which are only of the flesh,
nor was it sufficient to be satisfied with the miracle of the
loaves. The crowd was disappointed. They had dis-
cerned, at the cost of great pains, that he was the Son of
David, but when they discovered that Jesus did not have
any intention of leading an insurrection, they left him
and went away. Christ withdrew, also, from this party
of revolutionaries, and went away on a journey, until their
ardor should cool.

The biographers of Jesus pass over this point without
comment, but to me it is a significant fact.

On his return from that journey, he secretly visited the
eastern shores of the lake where many Greeks were living,
and upon this a crowd of four thousand came together.
I agree with the higher critics of Germany who hold that
it is a mistake to think that the same incident is reported
twice, in the stories of the feeding of the five thousand
and of the four thousand. It is interesting to note that the
group of five thousand later decreased to four thousand;
with the cooling of the fever of their enthusiasm, their
numbers decreased twenty per cent. But Jesus avoided
this second crowd and set out to roam about from place to
place.

It was at this time that the confession of Caesarea Phi-
lippi took place. Christ felt that because he had forsaken
the people, his popularity had decreased. So he asked
them, " Well, what does everyone think about me? I

suppose my popularity has suffered a good deal." His disciples replied that the crowd thought he was either John the Baptist, Elijah, Jeremiah, or one of the prophets. Then he asked, "And what do you think?" Peter answered, "You are the Son of God." "But you must not tell anyone now," replied Jesus. "I am soon to be crucified."

While the disciples had kept out of the revolutionary movement, yet they had the idea that at some other time they would lead a revolt, and they were greatly disappointed at the reply. Even then on the way home some of the disciples talked of nothing else but of becoming ministers of state in the kingdom. Jesus rebuked them by saying, "If anyone of you wishes to be great, let him become a servant." And again when the two sons of Zebedee wanted him to call down fire from heaven to destroy the Samaritans who would not let the Jews pass through their village, Jesus replied that he had not come to destroy but to save. And yet again he told the mother who requested that her two sons be made the chief ministers of state, "I have not come to command the service of others; I am on my way to death." Thereupon Judas in desperation was driven at length to treachery. But Christ demonstrated his teaching by himself washing his disciples' feet.

IT IS FINISHED

The material recorded by Matthew and Mark was furnished by Peter, and because he had fled, he did not know exactly what words Jesus spoke while on the Cross, with the exception of the cry, "Eloi, eloi, lama sabachthani." But there were women standing near the foot of the Cross, and Luke, basing his record on the account given by them, reports three utterances of Christ, in which he forgives the multitude, pardons the thief, and offers the prayer by which he commits his own spirit to God. As John stood with the women, he also reports three utterances, that is, the words whereby Jesus entrusted his mother to John, told of his thirst, and the final cry, " It is finished." Moreover, John comments on each word, saying, " that the Scripture might be fulfilled."

We should note carefully these words, " It is finished." What was finished? I think it means that the Christ who was in very truth the Christ, who had taken upon himself all suffering — who, as foretold in the fifty-third chapter of Isaiah, had borne all that had to be borne — had perfected his work. In direct contrast to the conception which the disciples held, that is, a messiah of worldly glory, he chose to be a Christ who endured suffering. " The hour is come that the Son of man should be glorified. Verily, verily I say unto you, except a grain of wheat fall into the ground, it abideth by itself alone, but if it die, it beareth much fruit." (John 12:23, 24.) Christ was to be glorified, not by turning to revolution, but by enduring the suffering of the Cross.

Even the Christian church of today misunderstands Christ here. The purpose of our having mystical experience is not that we may achieve our own personal satisfaction, but that we may succor the poor, help those who are in trouble, and educate the masses. If this were not Christ's teaching, we could not challenge the terrific power of this capitalistic civilization. If we are to allow this world to perish, we are not involved in any difficulties; but God loved this world enough to send his only Son. We are not to separate ourselves from the world; that is Buddhist teaching. We must keep on fighting until the very last slave, the last prostitute, is saved.

In the seventh century the Christian church allowed

idolatry to enter the church, and because of this mistake she was unable to withstand the onslaughts of Mohammedanism which began to invade the world. Because the church had permitted image worship to creep in, she had to bow before this low-grade, loveless religion, which is full of error. But Mohammedanism has no social consciousness, whereas the Old Testament makes the Hebrew race its center, and is full of the ideas of love and service. The tragedy still remains that there are two hundred million souls in this world today held captive by this religion whose foundation principle is conflict, simply because the Christian church was asleep.

Again in the nineteenth century, because the church had allowed itself to be absorbed in argument and theory, the masses threw it aside, and turned eagerly to communism. If we had had the love of St. Francis, they would never have turned to communism in this way. But sad to say, Christianity became dogma and ceased to be ethics. Therefore communism sprang up, which is identical with Mohammedanism in its being based on violence. Mohammedanism is still strong in China, where its followers band together and live a strongly communistic life. The Marxists, again, have a materialistic dialectic which is similar to that taught in the Koran. The Christian church has had to meet these crises because she practiced idolatry and because she lacked the practical expression of Christian love.

If the Christian church does not take note of this fact, and if she does not change her ways and actually practice Christian love, and thus meet the needs of the proletarian masses, a wave of Marxism will sweep over the world, which will capture hundreds of millions of people, and Christianity will have to submit to oppression for hundreds of years.

This was not Christ's way. He chose a religion of suffering and realized it by actually living it out.

FROM IDEAL TO ACTION

It is not enough to have ideals. We must translate them into action. The reason that Marxism attracts men is because it has the power to practice its teachings. Theology is all right, but there is no strength in a theology which does not become apparent in practice. This is the weakness of the nineteenth century. Together with the rapid advance in knowledge, there must be a living out of principles in action. In the parable of the judgment in the twenty-fifth chapter of Matthew, we learn that it is useless to protest that one has high ideals or a flair for the mystical. Those who are given a place among the righteous are those who help the poor to prosper, who visit those who are weeping in prison, who feed the hungry. Christ said that it was for such acts as these that those who have performed them are given a place among the good. It was not enough to say, " Lord, Lord," merely with the lips.

It comes down simply to this — it is not enough to be a nominal Christian. Look at the proletariat! Are they not suffering? We must do something to help them. How shall we take this parable? Do we not hear in it a solemn voice of warning?

DOCTRINE OR PRACTICE

The Middle Ages displayed two tendencies, the Franciscan and the Dominican. One movement arose in Italy, the other in Spain. The Franciscan made love actual in practice. The Dominican emphasized doctrine. The influence of these two movements is active in the world today. What, then, ought we to do? Should we live the

Christ-life in actual practice, or is it enough to subscribe to a doctrine? The only value that there is in doctrine is that it is an explanation of one's actions. It is easy enough to stay in one's study, but to live with beggars, and to associate with day-laborers, that is difficult. And while we shut ourselves up in our studies, the ideals of Marxism and Mohammedanism sweep the world with tremendous force, until the world is convulsed with violence.

God was actualized in the daily life of Jesus. We, too, must press forward along the path of Christ, which leads through suffering. I want to realize the suffering of the thousands of unemployed. Some of us who are working in connection with the Kingdom of God Movement are giving up one meal out of the twenty-one meals of a week and are sending the money to the unemployed. If all the people in the country were to give up a meal a week, all the unemployed could be helped. But because, like Peter, we try to flee from the Cross, violent revolution breaks out.

Let me tell you about one of my friends, Motoichiro Takahashi. He was formerly a minister of the Congregational Church in Japan. He came to Tokyo and began to distribute tickets for medical examination to the poor. When he graduated with first honors from the Doshisha middle school, his friend Senji Yamamoto held second place. When in later years Yamamoto was killed by a gangster, Takahashi said that he would take his revenge like a Christian, and went around distributing food tickets to the poor. He earned only a yen a day, and had work only once in a while, and at length even that work stopped. He moved into the top of a tenement in the Fukugawa slums. But even that did not satisfy him, and he began work for the people in the " Okan " district where there are many cheap lodging houses. In this district, the people who have no shelter build a fire and spend the night warming themselves around it. There are often seventy or eighty people encamped around the fire, and what is even worse, along the edge of the land which was being made at that time by filling in a shallow part of Tokyo bay, there were some who were even living in caves. He put up a tent, and took in these men. Some earnest Christians who were in the lumber business contributed some lumber at a very low figure to floor the tents, and with such help Takahashi was able to accommodate some three hundred men.

Because this was a practical demonstration of the true love of Christ, the Tokyo newspapers gave it publicity, and Matsui Sho-wo, a well-known playwright, wrote a play dramatizing it, and presented it on the stage at the Hibiya Public Hall. It was only a small thing to do, yet to put up the tents, to work among the men organizing temperance societies, and at the end to fall stricken by tuberculosis of the lungs, this was a valuable expression of Christ's love.*

Although we take the Cross upon our shoulders, we fail to bear it meekly and silently. I wish we might be ambitious to lead the life of the Cross in quietness. Let us examine ourselves to see whether we are leading the life of the Cross.

PRAYER

O God, our Father: We seek Thy guidance in this time of great economic change. We confess the sins of our age: that there is struggle between the capitalists and the proletariat in our society today; that there is strife between the peoples of different nations. The poor are wandering

* American readers may remember Mr. Takahashi as the peace poet, some of whose many poems on peace were published in the *Christian Century* and other journals soon after the Manchurian incident in the fall of 1931.

about our streets, and social work and social movements are powerless to help them. In truth, our hearts are filled with shame at the plight in which we find ourselves.

Teach us to meditate upon the life of Christ, and to remember how he threw his life away for the race of men. As we contemplate his passion and the blood which he shed, may Thy Spirit work deeply in our hearts. Strengthen us that we may live lives worth while, be it in ever so small a way. Inspired by the love of Christ, teach us to fling aside all desire for selfish advantage and for group privilege. Do Thou teach us, O Christ, to take up the Cross and to serve society. In the country, in fishing villages, on the sea, in the slums, on the streets, in the schoolroom, wherever Thou dost place us, deepen our resolution and cause us to bear the Cross and walk in Thy way. Do Thou use us, we pray, to Thy heart's content. In Christ we ask it. Amen.

XV

THE CROSS AND ETHICAL LIFE

That I may know Him, and the power of His resurrection, and the fellowship of His sufferings, being conformed unto His death. Philippians 3:10, 11.

THE Cross was not suicide. It was brought about by a strange providence, through the social forces of the day. It is recorded at the close of the eleventh chapter of John that the Council of Seventy Elders treated Christ as though he were a public nuisance; they announced publicly that they were seeking for him. This made possible the treachery of Judas Iscariot, who disclosed Jesus' whereabouts for a sum of money. But Christ could have fled, had he desired to do so. The Gospel of John is based upon material supplied by the administrative officials; read it to know the political causes of the Crucifixion. There are eight references in it to the killing of Jesus, or to the policy of suppression adopted towards him. (John 5:18; 7:1, 2; 7:3; 7:44; 8:59; 10:31; 10:39; 11:53.) In every recorded instance, Christ could have made his escape, had he chosen to do so.

For Christ was not merely a king. He founded his kingdom on love, not on strife. He chose the Cross because he had the Spirit of God which builds the Kingdom of God, and the will to bear the Cross. From a social viewpoint, therefore, he stands out, a king indeed.

But that is not all. Christ also holds a place as a

prophet in the ethical world. He was one of the prophets, and did his work from the prophetic point of view. He proclaimed a revision of the law of Moses. He was clearly conscious that he was greater than Solomon or Jonah. He was conscious of his own authority. " I say unto you," said he, " yet those who follow me will not entirely discard these former teachings."

It is easy to forget self-discipline when we are thinking only of society. When someone is watching us, we make an effort to improve ourselves, but when no one is looking at us, we relax our efforts. When we engage in social work, we are apt to fail in our inner life, to become ostentatious or to assume a pose, and thus to admit a serious shortcoming into the inmost depths of our nature. Christ did not fall short in this way. From the beginning to the end, he kept looking to the Cross. Socrates, Buddha, Confucius were all great men, but Christ was not simply a prophet-teacher like these men. He had the religious consciousness that as a high priest he must die for his people. This conviction led Christ to the Cross. Christ took his stand not as a moral critic, but as one possessing the consciousness of God, who purposes to save mankind.

Yet here I would like to discuss the moral teachings of Christ. He possessed a morality of the highest standard. Moreover, his morality was different from that of other men.

THE REVISION OF THE MOSAIC LAW

Christ's ethical teachings are of two types — the direct teachings, such as we find in the Sermon on the Mount, and the indirect teachings, such as are contained in the parables. In the direct teachings there are many precepts for individuals; here we find a revision of the teachings of Moses. On the other hand, the parables are for the most part social in their implications. The first four of the Ten Commandments have reference to our duties toward God, and the last six to our duties toward mankind. Christ revised this order first of all. The Sermon on the Mount begins with our duty to other men, and the teaching that we should walk the way with prayer and fasting does not appear until nearly the middle. Since God is our Father, we do not need to use many repetitions in worshipping him; when we worship him, we must carry in our hearts mercy and compassion. In this way Christ taught a revision of the Mosaic law from the religious viewpoint. Moses taught that one must respect one's father and mother, but Christ expounded the way of the " greater filial piety," that is, the love of God. Where the law taught, "Thou shalt not kill," he taught, "Do not be angry." With regard to the command, "Do not commit adultery," he warned men not to look at a woman with lustful desire. Instead of "Thou shalt not steal," he taught, "Give freely." In the place of "Do not bear false witness," he advised men to put themselves into the other's place. Instead of "Thou shalt not covet," he told them to surrender everything to God.

If this were all, Christ's teaching would not surpass other codes, for it would consist of a negative morality, teaching "Do not do this" and "Do not do that." It was when he said, "Love your enemy," that Christ's ethical revolution started. Not only did he revise the Mosaic law and make the moral life a matter of conscience; not only did he take that which was exterior and make it a matter of the inner life; the very foundation of his system is the will to save others, the great conviction that one must save his fellowmen. The feeling that one must save — that is, the feeling of the Cross — flows deep beneath it all.

Because one is eager to take up one's cross and help his

fellow, one can give the second mile of service; and when one is struck upon the right cheek, one is impelled to offer the other.

It is the ordinary thing to return evil for evil. There is no will to save in the " Way of Benevolence " of Confucius. I went to China in 1931, and while there I made a study of Confucius. I visited the ancestral shrine, and examined the records minutely. At forty-two Confucius became the Minister of Agriculture of the country of Ro, then the Minister of Justice, and when he was past sixty Prime Minister. Twice during that time he got rid of his enemies by killing them. His benevolence was unbending and unrelenting, and did not surpass that of the Old Testament. But Christ had the love which wills-to-save, and that sort of love is flexible.

Confucius standardized ordinary human customs; but Christ showed that if God's power reinforced that of man, a more than human will-to-save might bring about a life of daily love. Ordinarily this eludes our understanding. Not even a sparrow can fall to the ground but the Father permits it. How much more does his love seek to save the perishing! It was that love which Christ set forth. In every one of his teachings it is revealed.

SOCIAL ETHICS

The parables of Christ are of three types, and come from three periods in Christ's life. Each one of the three periods in Christ's ministry has its special characteristics; they are, the Galilean period, the Perean period, and the Judean period. The parables of the Galilean period, which are found in the fourth chapter of Mark and the thirteenth chapter of Matthew, reveal a creative spirit. The growth of the seed, the story of the spread of the leaven, the mustard seed, the story of the pearl, all put great emphasis on creative development. There is abounding energy, but the conscious desire to save is not yet clear.

But when Christ begins to look forward to the Cross, there is a sudden change in the tone of the parables. This is apparent in Luke. The story of the Good Samaritan in the tenth chapter, the parable of the fig-tree in the thirteenth chapter, the Prodigal Son in the fifteenth chapter, illustrate this new note.

The story of the Prodigal Son sets forth the beautiful foundation principle of redemption. The older brother has the unbending type of morality which Confucius teaches, and persists in treating bad people as bad. But the father welcomes the wrong-doer with tears of love, for his love is more flexible; and he says, " No, no, my son; let us forgive him." This demonstrates the difference between the ordinary run of simple morality and the morality of Christ. His morality is founded on a conscious desire to save others.

In the Perean period of Christ's ministry this redemptive element grows clearer as time progresses. If this element is missing, Christian teaching becomes pharisaical. It forgets to strive to save the wayward youth, the discharged prisoner, and others of that type. It attempts to evade the Cross. Are we not fleeing from the Cross? Are we not lacking in a conscious yearning to save others? Are we day by day bearing the burden of the sin of our families and our groups?

The parables of the Judean period teach that one should guard the precious values which have been previously won. The story of the servants who added to the value of the sums of money entrusted to them, the parable of the ten virgins, five of whom did not let their lights go out, the story of the tenants who refused to pay tribute, all teach the guarding or preservation of values. The parable of the practice of Christian love in the stern twenty-fifth chapter of Matthew is one of these, and furthermore, it contains within it a social ethic. In the twentieth chapter of Matthew, the story of the laborers in the vineyard, we find a great deal to help us in solving the problems of labor and of unemployment. It teaches that a minimum wage should be established first of all in order to give security of livelihood; and it teaches that work should be given to those who do not have it, and it guarantees equality of personality. When those laborers who were hired first complained that their wages were insufficient, and asked for more, the master rebuked them.

John Ruskin, in his essay, "Unto This Last," points out very clearly that this principle, the equal value of each individual, more than any other, is the Christian solution of the problem. But the one who has made a study of this principle, and has taken his stand on it, is Gandhi. The most worthless person, even a beggar, is a child of God, and therefore we must guard and preserve his life, his work, and his personality. But are we doing this? Are we giving life and work and character to those who labor?

The practice of the parables must be upon the Cross as a foundation. Individualistic precepts do not remain individualistic in them, but point the way to the redemption of society. In this these parables surpass the teachings of Buddha, of Confucius and Socrates. In that it boldly ventures that which cannot be accomplished without God, Christ's morality is eternally young, new, and indestructible.

CRIME AND SALVATION

In 1931 I took supper one evening with Shumpei Homma, and asked him how it was that he had devoted his life to the care and education of delinquents and ex-convicts. He told me that he used to be a jinricksha man in the city of Wakamatsu in Aizu prefecture. One day a judge of the Appellate Court from Tokyo fell asleep over the book he had been reading while riding along in the jinricksha, and dropped it in the mud. When Homma picked it up and tried to give it back to him, he said it was so soiled he did not want it, so Homma asked him for it and took it home with him. The book was in English and he could not read it. Still he wanted so much to read it that he began the study of English, starting from A, B, C, and wrestling with a dictionary. With all his might and main he studied the book. It was a copy of Lombroso's *Criminology,* and in it the opinion was set forth that murderers are physiologically different from other men, and that in the case of criminals the bones of the skull show that there is not the slightest hope that these men can ever improve.

As Homma read the book, he felt that Lombroso could never have written in that way if he had ever lived with criminals, and he conceived a great desire to try for himself to live with criminals in order to prove that this theory was wrong. So he made his way to Tokyo and finally retired to a quiet place called Akiyoshidai in Yamaguchi prefecture, to give himself to his work for wayward youths.

It may be that from the standpoint of criminology, criminals are physiologically different from other men, and cannot become better men. But from Christ's standpoint, they can be saved. The reason that prayer-meetings have grown musty is because we have ceased to believe in the power of God which can save. We do not sincerely believe in prayer. We only pray for those things which we are obliged to pray for. We do not ask the

Lord to save the one hundred and sixty thousand criminals who crowd our prisons; we do not ask God for the two million seven hundred thousand delinquent boys and girls that the problem of delinquency may be wiped out. We temporize by praying for things which are inconsequential. We pray for trivial things, regarding which it makes little difference whether we pray or not. Christ must enter more deeply into our experience, and we must pray with deep conviction. Is it not written that prayer is inevitably answered? Christ went through with his death upon the Cross courageously because he believed that salvation could be made complete. He was convinced of the moral efficacy of salvation. We must pray with faith, though others may think us superstitious.

Juji Ishii always had three diaries. He was always looking back to the diary of last year and the year before that, to see how many of his prayers were being answered during the current year, and he kept a diary of thanksgiving to record his answered prayers. The mats on the floor in the corner of the room where he knelt in prayer every day were worn down into a little hollow. It was this firm belief in prayer that sustained his large orphanage.

There are some who criticize the Kingdom of God Movement, and say scornfully, " How can a million souls be saved? " But if we were to pray we would be given a million souls. God is ready to give Japan these million souls but we lack the conscious intention of saving these souls, and of taking up our Cross and bearing it, as we go along our way.

We do not read our Bibles in sober earnest. Let us become conscious of the fact that we are lacking in faith, that we are not bearing the Cross. Let us attach importance once more to our church prayer-meetings. Let us remember and believe that Christ promised that where two or three gathered together, he would be there with them. With our hearts full of a conscious will to save others, let us walk the way with earnest prayer. It is because we pray that we are able to turn the right cheek when we are struck upon the left cheek.

Inosuke Inouye started out to evangelize the Formosan aborigines who had killed his father. His friends were ready to help him, but a certain governor-general would not give his support to the plan, saying that it was impossible to save such people; the only thing to do was to wipe them out. Therefore every year Japan spends four million yen for military equipment and men to hold only a hundred and thirty thousand aborigines under control. This is the fundamental mistake of the policy of suppression. Why have they not spent the same amount of money in sending missionaries to these people, and in showing them kindness?

In Scotland they claim that if workers are added to the staff of the Salvation Army, the police department can safely decrease its force. I wish that we, too, could work with all our might for the poor and the criminal, as though we too were Salvation Army workers. We should be pouring out our energy, praying as we work, and believing in prayer, to save Japan and to plant the ethical teaching of the Cross firmly in our country. Let us pray that the Holy Spirit may work within the enfeebled churches to this end.

PRAYER

O God our Father: Forgive us that we have not fully realized what agony Christ endured to manifest his love towards us. Help us to exert ourselves, as Christ did, for

the sake of the people. Teach us to struggle on, like brave
soldiers who, though covered with blood, keep fighting des-
perately. Grant unto us that we may discover the blood-
stained Cross in the factory, in the highways, in the shops,
by living lives of loyal service. And this we pray in
Christ. Amen.

XVI

THE CROSS AND RELIGIOUS LIFE

If any man would come after me, let him deny himself, and take up his cross, and follow me. Matthew 16:24.

JESUS was a king, a priest, and a prophet. From the modern viewpoint there were three aspects to his work, the social, the ethical, and the religious. It is not sufficient to meditate upon the Cross in its social and ethical aspects. It is only when we consider the religious aspect of the Cross that we get down to fundamentals.

The social movements of our day can understand the first two of these aspects of the Cross but they cannot appreciate the religious consciousness of the Cross. Men of this modern age are particularly apt to hold redemption in derision. They phrase their doubts in the following questions: Can one man make atonement for another? Can the efforts of the past become an atonement for the present age? How can the effort of an individual effectively atone for the crimes of society? Christ said in the twentieth chapter of Matthew, and again in the twenty-sixth, that his blood would become a ransom for many, to save many from their sins, but there is a tendency in this present day to ignore redemption. We must understand this tendency. It is a consequence of the fact that our age does not regard sin as seriously as did the age of Christ.

Religious consciousness develops together with the development of conscience. Therefore, when there is no keen sense of conscience, such conceptions as the redemptive power of the Cross become impossible. If one studies the books of Exodus, Deuteronomy, and Hebrews, one can understand how the worship of the Judean people was a type of that which was to come. The religious consciousness is not yet fully developed but it has come to life, and has produced an archetype of the perfected religious consciousness. At first the Hebrews were satisfied with a system of sacrifices and of burnt-offerings. Up to the present time, Japan has not produced this solemn sacrifice of an offering for sin, or for trespass, offered because of one's own sin. There is only a hazy and undeveloped conception of this kind, in the recognition of the six roots of evil, the eyes, the ears, the nose, the tongue, the body and the mind; and we find also the feeling of the need for their purification. When we examine the New Testament, we find the idea of conscience has become more fully developed and the conscious will-to-redeem glows like a spark of living fire in its pages. The realization that one must bear the burden of the sins of men in the past, in the present, and in the future becomes a strong and powerful conviction.

THE DEVELOPMENT OF THE RELIGIONS
OF ANTIQUITY

The Greek religion followed the same line of development. Why should Greece, which had produced so many philosophers, have had to take over the religion of the Jews? Gilbert Murray, in his book on *The Four Periods of Greek Religion*, discusses this question. In olden times men were so lacking in religious consciousness that one could kill another without the slightest concern. In these modern days we attribute everything to environment and are equally without a sense of concern. No matter what a man may do, he is nonchalant. This is the reason that the idea of redemption is incomprehensible today.

Greece also, like our modern age, was absorbed in the pursuit of pleasure. First they worshipped Zeus, and then they took up as the next step the worship of Apollo. They then developed the Delphic Shrine as a place where they could have their sins atoned for. From this they progressed to the idea that they must be born anew in order to be saved from their sins. For this reason the worship of Dionysius was introduced, and we find carvings of Zeus carrying the small babe Dionysius in his arms. The small babe represents the idea of re-birth and this conception can be traced to Persia from which it originated. Gradually there arose the powerful hope that a Savior, that is, a Christ who would be more than human, and not merely a man, should be born. The philosophy of Socrates and Plato had stirred the religious consciousness of men, and men longed for this Christ to come. The Greeks could not be satisfied with Socrates or Plato but awaited the Christ. The time was ripe.

The Egyptian religion developed in much the same way. The religion of the descendants of Ham and Shem changed with the development of conscience just as religion had changed with the Greeks. Together with the awakening of conscience, men's hearts began to ache over their past sins, and just as the injury of a part will arouse pain throughout the whole body, so the conscience began to cause distress to the hearts of men because of the sins of the human race. The poison had penetrated throughout the whole body, and the pain was intolerable. This longing for a Savior, for re-birth, was the inevitable outcome of the long experience of the human race. The buds of Old Testament truth blossomed out into flowers in New Testament times.

THE ACT OF ATONEMENT

The consciousness of the Cross lay hidden in Christ's heart even from the very beginning of the Galilean period of his preaching. Over and over again he told his disciples that he had come not to be served by men, but to serve them; that he had come not to judge men, but to save them. But they did not grasp his teaching in the least. Because he thought his disciples would not understand his death, he explained to them the work of the Holy Spirit. " My act is in accordance with the Scriptures," said he. " It is an act of redemption. Since you do not understand now, let yourselves be taught by the Holy Spirit, which God will send you at that time." If Jesus had not taken up the Cross, and borne it, his message would have had no meaning.

If the Sermon on the Mount is taken by itself alone, Christ's teaching is not so very different from that of the sages of China. The real point of difference between the teachings of Christ and these sages is that even at the instant when Christ was hanging on the cross, he loved his enemies and prayed for them. If one is looking merely for ethical precepts, it is not necessary to go to Christ. In saving men from all their past sins, in taking all the past failures of men, and re-shaping their lives once more anew, in giving them the capacity for growth and development, Christ entered into the conscious will-to-redeem, which fills the heart of God, and in this spirit did his priceless work.

I once knew a man who had killed another, and he was in constant torment, saying that the ghost of his victim kept haunting him. Even though such a man has been pronounced " not guilty " by the court, and his case thus settled by society, still his conscience does not forgive him. When one meets with a man like this, there is no other way to comfort him but to tell him, " You can be at peace, for Christ died for that sin." Those who quibble and criticize this as superstition will not be satisfied with it, but what other salvation is there for such a man? I have seen many such men, and for this reason I have come to hold a theory of atonement which is not based on theology or philosophy.

Christ did not die upon the Cross because of some philosophical or theological theory. He poured out his love in response to the groans of the souls of men. When one accepts this work of Christ's with sincerity and simple gratitude, and with a meek submissive spirit, one can be saved. Where is there in history any other man who has thus sincerely grieved over the sins of men, and yearned to save them? By having a complete consciousness of sin, such a consciousness as God has, he brought salvation to perfection. One who does not consciously share this redemptive purpose of God cannot imagine one's responsibility towards God. We are always running away. Our consciences give us no rest when we realize that we ought to shoulder our responsibility to the uttermost. It is Christ and he alone who in all the world of men thought the thing through, and then said, " I will take it all upon myself. I will take all the responsibility for all sin upon my own shoulders."

Here is a heroic conscience! We hear all sorts of stories of troubled conscience. Is there any true comfort which we can offer other than this, " The blood of Christ, by God's grace, will atone for all your sins "? There has never been another in all history save Christ who brought to its consummate perfection the love which purposes to save men.

THE CONVERSION OF PAUL AND
HIS GRASP OF ATONEMENT

Christ's disciples did not understand the meaning of the atonement at all. It was not until Paul appeared that it was understood, and by Paul only with difficulty. Paul was at first very much opposed to Christ. He thought it disgraceful to worship in such superstitious fashion the carpenter Jesus, a political revolutionary, and he opposed the new cult in manly fashion, combing every corner of the country in order to persecute its believers. But no matter how bitterly he fought it, Christ's teaching continued to spread. As there were continually those from among his own friends who were becoming Christians, he gradually became uneasy as to his own actions. And then one day, as he was walking along a road, with his heart full of uncertainty, a vision of Christ appeared to him, and he heard a voice in his ear: " Saul, Saul, why are you persecuting me? " When Paul asked, " Who are you? " he was told, " I am the Christ whom you persecute." He was unable to see for three days and three nights, and only when something like scales fell from his eyes was he at length able to see again.

I have had a similar experience. At one time I was unable to see for forty-five days, and a scale-like substance was removed from my eyes.

Through this experience Paul realized that the Cross of Christ was lifted up for the sake of manifesting the redemptive love of God: that this was why Christ died. Sin is death. When we become the slaves of sin, we lose our strength. We are sold as slaves. Or again our development is arrested; we become depraved; we wander from the way; we miss the mark. Because we have broken the law, we must have the sentence "Not guilty: set at liberty," pronounced upon us. By the Cross we are released from slavery and given freedom; we return again to life and become heirs of God. Having grasped the fact that Christ died in order to save us, we realize that we are, each one of us, the very chief of sinners, that we are such criminals as to have repaid God's mercy with enmity.

In this way Paul enters into the feelings of Christ; he tells us that he has clearly experienced Christ's feelings in such passages as Colossians 1:24, and Philippians 1:29. It was his purpose to take up for himself the work of Christ and to carry it on and to complete in time the sufferings of Christ which were lacking. Not satisfied with his own redemption, he began to work for even the material salvation of others. Individualistic religion was not enough for him, and he became an expert in helping and evangelizing the poor. (Galatians 2:10.) In the seventh and eighth chapters of II Corinthians we see how he loved the poor and that it was his plan to give them aid. But he was misunderstood when he tried to do others this kindness, and all sorts of things were said about him. Nevertheless, all his life long he was a self-supporting evangelist. It was when he had gone to Jerusalem to take a gift of money for the poor that he was finally taken prisoner.

It is impossible to restrict the gospel of Christ to narrow limits. It redeems the sins of the past, restores the present, and stimulates development in the future. Moreover, this is not merely in the case of the individual, but for society as well. We must conceive of it as the liberation of the entire human race. The gospel is the message of a year of jubilee, of a year of rejoicing. It should mean the liberation economically, politically, socially, physiologically and spiritually of the human race. It must mean the true emancipation of the whole of humanity.

There is a tendency to make the gospel into an innocuous, non-committal sort of thing. But we should make it thorough-going and complete salvation to those who are in prison, to the poor, to those who are weakened by illness, to the unemployed. We must not think of Christ's blood as shed for the sake of the individual. We must not believe in a salvation for one's self alone, a salvation of selfish advantage, drawing water off to one's own rice-fields. The salvation of the whole human race and the whole of society must be our goal.

PRAYER

O God our Father: Forgive us that we do not clearly understand how to walk in the footsteps of Christ, though with our lips we name His name. We take Thy name upon our lips in prayer, and do not deeply grasp His teachings. We confess our easy-going indifference. We confess that because our lives are not filled with the conscious desire to save others, we have not perceived that Christ, the Christ who was worthy to be the Son of God, this Christ who saves us, is offering his blood to wipe away the stains which come from the gaping wounds of the hearts of men. Teach us the many things we should learn from the example of Christ. O reveal to us now, with radiant clearness, the Christ who passed through the death upon the Cross in order to redeem us. When we are sad, when we are criticized by others unkindly, when our hearts are burdened with greed, teach us to fix our eyes upon the God-like figure of Christ, who refused to depend upon violence or force, or to return evil for evil. Lead us forward upon our path, we pray, in the name of our Savior. Amen.

XVII

THE CROSS AND DAILY LIFE

From that time Jesus began to show his disciples that he must go unto Jerusalem, and suffer many things of the elders and chief priests and scribes, and be killed, and the third day be raised up. Matthew 16:21.

And he said unto all, If any man would come after me, let him deny himself, and take up his cross daily, and follow me. Luke 9:23.

IT IS easy for the Japanese people to understand the conception of God, but it is hard for them to grasp the Cross. They may speak glibly of the Cross, but there are few who really understand it, and fewer still who practice it. It is particularly true of men of this modern age that they do not grasp the meaning of the Cross, nor do they live the life of the Cross in any thorough-going fashion. The civilization of this present day is in exact opposition to the Cross, for it makes self the center, and puts its claims first. Because the people of the present day take the position that if one's own class or one's own nation is getting along well, that is quite enough, we find widespread unrest among the oppressed, and the right to live, the right to labor, the rights of personality are defended with bitterness and desperation. Such movements as communism and socialism, which are not founded upon

the Cross, take the attitude that it makes no difference
what happens to others if only a man has work for himself. It is of no importance what happens to the rich —
let him be out of work, let the landowner be out of employ-
ment; who cares? Let the proletarians work to establish
the position of their own class, no matter what happens to
the landlords! The fate of those who live on land rents
is quite unimportant! Of course, the Cross is unintelligible to such people.

There are at least five points of significance in the
Cross. In the first place, the Cross teaches us that whatever suffering may come is sent by God. If we feel that
suffering comes through other men, it becomes intolerable;
but we can accept it gladly if it is from God. Our modern
thought does not agree with this at all. There is a general
feeling that it is ridiculous to think of God as sending
suffering. It has no meaning, it is suffering, and nothing
more; as such it is to be avoided. Let us spend each day
as it comes in pleasure and enjoyment of life.

We have the habit in Japan of running away from
suffering. We have degenerated since the days of Hojo
when the Zen sect taught self-discipline and an austere
mode of life. When some great catastrophe, like the
earthquake, happens, our lack of vigor and spirit comes
to light. I have been told that there are a million or more
Koreans who have emigrated to northeastern Manchuria
because they have been dispossessed of their country.
They are enduring the trials of the cold climate with courage; although the summer is short, still they manage to
cultivate many acres of land, and even to grow some rice.
But the Japanese are always looking for an easy mode of
life, and they have lost the desire to persevere in enduring hardships. They are attempting to flee from the
Cross. (Philippians 3:18.)

If you complain that Japan is limited in extent, there is the northern island of the Hokkaido with over one million acres of uncultivated land; there is still plenty of room for people to immigrate there. The Hokkaido can take care of five times the population of the main island. There is Southern Saghalin (Karafuto) with its three hundred thousand acres of land, if one has the spirit to go as a colonist, to live simply and to work hard. The reason that the Japanese do not go in and occupy such lands is because they lack the willingness to endure privations, the spirit of bearing a cross. We must lay more stress upon this spirit.

When the disciples of Christ begged him to become their king, he deliberately chose instead the suffering of the Cross. In the thirteenth century during the Hojo period of Japanese history, there was a man called Eizai who taught Japan this way of suffering. He was a priest in the temple of Fudasan, belonging to the Zen sect, and he was a man of simple sincerity of spirit and vigor of character. It was this same spirit of simple frugality which occasioned many of the stories told of the heroes of that period, of Matsushita Zeni, and of Fujitsuna Aoto, who dragged the river to recover a copper coin — though it cost him more than the value of the coin — in order to restore it to circulation. It is told of Aoto that he took only the simplest fare, and the only relish he would take with his wine was *yake-miso,* a sort of toasted bean cake. Many other tales are told of him, which reveal a simple frugality of life almost religious in its atmosphere.

We moderns lack this atmosphere. The Hojo family had more of this tone than the Ashikaga or Tokugawa families, who succeeded them. Take, for example, Toki-yori Hojo, who when he was still a young man retired to the seclusion of a small temple, called Saimyoji, north of

Yokohama, and built himself a hut and took up the simple
and strictly ordered life of the Zen sect. In order to
discipline himself and to develop courage, he would rise
early in the morning for meditation; he lived on the
simplest of food, taking only a bowl of bean soup with
his rice; and he wore the gloomy black robes of the priests.
Tokiyori was succeeded by Tokimasa, and it was during
the latter's rule that Kublai Khan invaded Japan. It is
truly remarkable that Japan was able to resist this invasion, and in my opinion it is due to the influence of the
Zen sect, with its system of self-discipline and its emphasis on a simple, austere mode of life.

According to Mrs. E. A. Gordon, who visited Japan,
the Daruma, or famous Buddhist saint of Japan, was a
foreigner.* Mrs. Gordon felt that there was so much of
the element of the early Christian teaching in the train-
ing and discipline of the Zen sect that she claimed that
Daruma must have been either St. Thomas, the disciple
of Christ, or one of his followers. The virility of the
Kamakura period of Japanese history was due to the
spiritual discipline practised at that time. The reason
that the disciples of Christ conquered Europe was because
they had the will to trample suffering under their feet.
Unless the Japanese people have more of this spirit, Japan
cannot make progress. Instead of trying to imitate the
West, and doing it badly, it would be much better for us
to study and understand clearly the way of Christ, whose
origin was in Asia.

We who are followers of Christ must guard his secret.
We must have the secret skill of turning every pain into

* Daruma, the Buddhist saint of Japan, is known to Western students
of Buddhism by his Indian name of Bodidharma. He is ordinarily sup-
posed to have been an Indian Buddhist sage who migrated to China as a
Buddhist missionary.

joy. The only thing which brought the country through the crisis of the Hojo period was spiritual force. In our modern times, however, the individualistic religion of the Zen sect is inadequate. Many of the characteristic teachings of the Zen sect are to be found in Christianity, as well, but there must be group activity, too.

THE CONQUEST OF SORROW

In the second place, the Cross is a way of conquering sorrow. Not suffering alone but sorrow also is the lot of man. Suffering and sorrow may seem to be closely related, but there is a slight difference between them. Though a man may have a secure livelihood, he may be sad. Though he may have a lovely home and a good wife, and everything he needs, still that man may be sad. Some men are saddened by their lack of education; others are dissatisfied with life. Some meet with business failure. Shaka was born in a king's palace but he grieved over his environment which to others seemed so fortunate. Suffering is negative and sorrow is positive. The Cross is the way of conquest over sorrow. When one loses a child, one may not suffer in his own body, but as a parent he experiences sorrow. Although he tries to give up his child and resign himself to his loss, yet he cannot do it. Madame S—— was a countess, whose family belonged to the Nichiren sect. When she was in deep distress because of the loss of her child, she came to know the Way of Christ, which conquers sorrow. She suddenly awakened to the new truth and accepted Christian teaching. The teachings of Christianity make it possible to endure sorrow with a heart at peace.

When Jesus was being led away to the cross, a crowd of women followed him weeping. The road along which Christ was taken is called the Via Dolorosa today and stories have gathered around it. Christ told the weeping women to mourn rather over the day of destruction which would come to them. (Luke 23:27-31.) I am much impressed by the way in which Christ forgot his own suffering and thought only of the suffering of others. We must discover the secret of this composure which can forget its own sufferings and suffer for others. Although the Japanese people should be strong in meeting suffering, still there are few who meet its blows with self-possession.

Tom Sawyer, the hero of Mark Twain's famous novel, was a mischievous youngster, but for all his mischief, he was not a bad boy. The story is laid in the years when the basin of the Mississippi River was being reclaimed, and this ragged little rascal wanders about from one place to another, meeting with all sorts of adventures. He is without a friend, but he has learned to endure the sorrow of loneliness with composure. He is an ultra-modern boy. In Japan if a boy is mischievous, he is sure to be bad, but we still find this spirit of boyish innocent mischief in America today. The Americans are disorderly; I was amazed to see students in a university putting their feet up on their desks while listening to a lecture. But this spirit of nonchalance has its value, for it enables one to pass through suffering triumphantly. It seems to me that these people who have subjugated the immense continent of America are the world's prize lovers of fun. The Japanese are too fond of formality and ceremony and are too much inclined to put on airs of elegance. We must go back to the real spirit of the tea-ceremony, and find joy in even a sip of tea. I wish we might grasp and hold fast the spirit which is able to surmount every sorrow.

Livingstone had this spirit; he met suffering triumphantly. He trampled it under foot. Livingstone was not clever at preaching sermons. He chose the most difficult place in the world for his work, darkest Africa. He endured all sorts of suffering during the thirty years of his work; his friends said he was insane; he was separated by death from the wife he loved, but he kept on, pressing forward all the time. He was truly an incarnation of the spirit of Christ. He was thoroughly versed in geology, zoology, botany, and natural science and yet, with all his learning, he was so tender-hearted that he even loved the slaves. I like his virility, and his unflinching persistence during these thirty years. Young men in these modern times do not have the spirit even to bore a hole with an awl. I wish we might stir one another up to undertake the most difficult or disagreeable tasks; though others may dislike and avoid them, let us undertake them joyfully.

THE CONQUEST OF DEATH

The third significance of the Cross is the conquest of death. There are two meanings in death; the death of the body, physical death, and the death of the self. When we speak of death, we immediately think of physical death. Everyone is averse to death, but Christ sought out death and went his way to the Cross. When Jesus was on his second journey he said, " I will die in a short time," showing that he had included death in the program of his life. He also said that he would come to life again. When one can be as thorough-going as this, the sorrow in death evaporates. When we feel as though we would like to live forever, death becomes a sorrow, but when we put it in our program right from the start, it becomes a joy. Death becomes part of one's mission, one's allotted task.

Why did God create death? Death has first the meaning of elimination, and second, it provides a way that the self may prolong its existence and continue to grow. We look forward to death as the immigrants to Brazil look forward to life in the new country. In order that we might find in death the significance of a migration, Christ said that in his Father's house there were many dwelling places. Again he spoke of death as entrusting his soul to God. When we meditate on this meaning of death, we are not saddened by the fact of it.

THE CONQUEST OF SELF

The second meaning of death is the death of the self. We may understand the meaning of physical death very clearly but the death of self is much more difficult to grasp. We find these words, "having slain the enmity," in the sixteenth verse of the second chapter of Ephesians. Besides our physical selves we have certain instincts. Although from the standpoint of our conscious selves we desire to do those things which are good, yet we are also inclined to follow our instincts blindly, and the self is divided into two selves. One self wants to do the good, the other self, the self of instinct, which clings to the physical, longs to do evil. When we study Christ's prayer in Gethsemane, we find him abandoning himself utterly to God until his will is conformed exactly to the will of God. We find the two selves struggling in conflict in Paul, but in Christ the self of instinct had been put to death, and the self which consciously willed to suffer had conquered. The willingness to suffer shines out bright and clear. The prayer of Gethsemane reveals that although Christ felt an instinctive desire to live, still he would not selfishly ask for life. Christ prayed this prayer three times, and in the end he joyfully and resolutely cast aside the instinctive self, for the self of instinct has missed its way. It carries a load of sin, of lust, of dishonesty, of falsehood, of physical heredity and social heredity, which from God's viewpoint is enmity to him. All this Christ resolutely flung aside. This is the Cross.

God enters into our heart when we pray this prayer, and destroys all that is unsightly in our hearts, all the enmity, all the instincts; and death truly takes place, the death which strips off and throws aside the self, refusing to make request for any selfish advantage. Then for the first time the soul is born again into the life where one's will is one with God's will. This is the meaning of baptism. The old instincts fade away and new instincts come into play, instincts which are beautiful because they conform to the thoughts and feelings of God.

THE CONQUEST OF SIN

The fifth significance of the Cross is the forgiveness of sin. Up to this point we have been looking at the cross from the standpoint of mankind, but here we are looking at it from God's standpoint. Christ completed the burial of his self and then entered into the realm of God. Mankind, let us say, can progress to a certain point. In order that man may reach yet higher to another stage, it is necessary that God should say, " I will forgive everything which has gone before." This willingness on God's part is revealed in the Cross. Those who have come to Christ are saved by virtue of Christ's deeds and conquer death — the self, sorrow, suffering, all — in him. This is the forgiveness of sins. While it is a wonderful thing to feel that one is pardoned if one believes in Christ, it is not enough only to be saved oneself. It is not enough to repeat some such prayer as " Namu, Amida Butsu! " (Save us, O Buddha!)

Christianity is to believe in the Cross of Christ, and

then suffering and sorrow, death, and even selfishness, are conquered. The race has been saved through this revelation of God-like love. Christ hung on the Cross, moreover, because as he said the sin of the human race was an offense to God. In this sense Christ's Cross is a Cross of victory. It is a Cross which causes man in death to be resurrected to God. The Cross is the crystallization of the love of God. If a character such as Christ's appears, man's failures can be forgiven. Looking at the Cross we can discern the great love of God to man. Though we dwell in prison, in some lonely colony of emigrants, or in a world of sorrow through being misunderstood, we can trample under foot every difficulty, for we live in the conviction that God forgives. This is the acme of religion. This is the secret of Christianity.

PRAYER

O God of Heaven and Earth: We thank Thee that nineteen hundred years ago Thou didst reveal the perfect figure for mankind in the person of a carpenter. Through his courage, through his pity, his love of his fellowmen and his victory over suffering, sorrow, selfishness and sin, and death, Thou didst manifest to us the perfect man. Teach us that our own pathways of life must lead on into the Way of Christ who hung upon a Cross. Wavering, unwilling to make the choice, we hesitate. We humbly confess it. Cause the spirit of Christ to dwell in us, that we may kill selfishness, and be children of God who love our fellowmen. This we pray in the name of Christ. Amen.

XVIII

THE CROSS AND SOCIAL MOVEMENTS

*These are they that follow the Lamb whithersoever
he goeth, These were purchased from among men,
to be the first-fruits unto God and unto the Lamb.*
Revelations 14:4.

ALTHOUGH the Roman empire had been greatly influenced by the movement initiated by Jesus Christ, when it was invaded by the Huns, a barbarian race which swept down from western China, it was not able to withstand the invasion. When Christian love proved unable to conquer the spears of the barbarians, the Emperor Justinian worked out a system of laws which accepted Christian principles only in part and tried to blend force and love. Modern law is based upon this law of Justinian. In England, for instance, love is adopted as the law of the home, to some extent as the law of the country, but even in this peace-loving country, barbarian practices are still the rule in foreign relations.

Why is it that Europe, where Christianity is familiar, still engages in war? It is because Europe is only half-Christian. Kenneth Saunders once said: " There is more than one kind of Englishman; Englishmen are both pirates and angels." Ever since the time of Justinian, we find these two elements, love and force, in the laws and customs of every country which has developed a system of government. The nations of the world present a double face; from one view they are angels, from the other, devils. The nations of our present time are Justinian. Not one of them is out-and-out Christian. Germany, England and America are "Christian" countries, but one side of the picture of their world is dreadful. In Japan we too have a similar world of terrible inconsistencies.

Individually we are also facing in the two directions. The instincts are blind. They want to go to the night club, to drink and to "see life." The conscious self wants to know God, to walk in the path of righteousness. Man has these two tendencies in his nature. Paul states this clearly. He calls the self which longs to become like God the "new" man and the instinctive self the "old" man.

Within us there is the instinctive self and also the conscious one. Caught between these two, we are in trouble indeed. Just as the Roman Empire was distressed by the conflict between these two, we of today are also suffering, and have made little progress beyond that day. True culture makes consciousness its foundation, and rejects instinctive, reckless, and blind thinking. That is why I challenge our age to awaken to full consciousness. With the conscious mind man has been wanting to follow God and Christ, but has not been able to do so because of his instincts. In the West these two tendencies have been apparent.

In the midst of that confusion a young man emerged in Assisi of Italy. He was a knight, handsome, gifted, skilful in making friends, given to sport and to sowing his wild oats. Until eighteen he was a prodigal son, but then he made a hard and fast resolution never again to surrender to blind instinct, and began a valiant endeavor to become a child of God. His name was Francis.

Endeavoring to enter into the Christ-life, he meditated on the Cross as the deepest and highest symbol of love. And they say that the marks of the Cross appeared upon his own breast. This is a famous story. After that Italy could not free itself from his influence. Wherever I went in Italy, the Roman Catholic churches did not have pulpits to preach in, but were places for worship. On their altars is the Cross, and behind it a picture, and usually one of Francis. In the cathedral of Milan, for instance, a magnificent marble temple big enough to hold a congregation of ten thousand, is a picture of him by Giotto. It is said that no other person has ever entered so thoroughly into the life of love which Christ lived, as St. Francis. Buddhism in Japan has been influenced by him. Nishida Tenko is a person who has tried to live a life like that of Francis. And among the Buddhists, Shinran Shonin, Ryokan, and others have lived lives similar to his.

What was it which transformed this wayward youth, who found the days too short to satisfy his craving for pleasure and for power, into a lover of little birds, a lover of nature, a lover of humanity? This noble personality was entirely the work of the Cross. We can discover the pure grace of God in a conversion as thoroughgoing as this one. We of this modern age ought to experience this sort of conversion.

We can study the Cross from many different aspects. We can consider the Cross as a social principle, for there must be a spirit of sacrifice if society is to advance. Again we may consider the Cross from the educational viewpoint, or from the standpoint of the emotions. The enthusiasm which the Cross inspires is a marvelous thing. When one meditates on the Cross, centering one's attention on it, what emotion sweeps through our souls! It is the Cross which gives us strength to endure sorrow and suffering! It is the Cross which urges us on and challenges us to moral adventure! We are lost in adoration when we contemplate the scheme of life which is revealed in the Cross.

THE PLAN OF LOVE

Let us study the Cross as the principle of love. Man is part devil and part angel; he is capable of conscious choice, and at the same time he is a creature of blind instinct. I would like to let our minds dwell on the fact that, as children of God, we are able to grasp the fundamental meaning of the Cross for us, as his children. There is only one foundation principle; that is, love.

We think of love as like a longing for one's loved one, and indeed, the differentiation of sex takes its origin in this deep foundation principle of the universe. The universe is divided into male and female in order that the world may go on. The reason that amoebae do not evolve into something higher is because they reproduce by fission; new amoebae split off from the parent amoeba. But if you wish progress, there must be differentiation of sex. There had to be this marvelous arrangement of male and female in order to provide a starting point for the awe-inspiring process of evolution. God planned that his universe should progress through the human race, and in that plan love has its part.

In Christianity, therefore, the problem of sex is met in a reverent attitude because it arises out of the fundamental law of evolution, which is in turn a fundamental principle of the universe. Here we are in sympathetic accord with Jesus Christ, who said that a man would leave his father and mother and cleave to his wife and they would become one. Christianity reverences marriage. It respects marriage and holds the highest ideals for it. Formerly Christianity was disliked because of its insistence on a high standard of morality, but it is generally recognized today that this principle of sex morality is a fundamental principle of development and progress. If we have a good heritage we are capable of progress to the point of becoming saints; yet because we take our ease before we reach the goal, we lose strength and power and retrogress. This is sin. We are inclined to think of sin as the infraction of some moral law, such as stealing, but it is sin for us, who should become the children of God, to be caught in a giddy whirl and cease to progress.

When, over and above that, our heredity is tainted by alcoholism, or with syphilis, the problem becomes even more complicated. For this reason there is nothing so sacred as the relations between the sexes. We should keep them as pure as though we were in God's presence. We should abandon all licentiousness. We must not treat sex as though it were half a joke. Hidden within these mysteries is God's plan. It is not merely human love; it is God's love. We must become fully aware of this. God created the universe in such a way that it might progress through this love of God revealed to the human race.

That love keeps spreading out to society. It becomes sex-love, friendship, patriotism, and at last the love of the whole of society. All this is God's design. If love between the sexes sets forward the evolution of the universe, so does the love of society as a whole. All must put love into practice, working together with good will, each making his particular contribution towards the reorganization of society. Whether it be bookkeeping or an intellectual contribution, we must make our love thoroughgoing. We must learn to practice Christian love in our economic systems, in the educational world, in social matters, in every phase of life.

It is easy to understand this when we look at the educational world. No one individual can build up a university. One person studies optics, and produces a magnifying-glass. Another makes a study of atoms through that magnifying-glass. Another discovers some new truth about the cells of the brain, and thus there is advance. If there is selfishness, there is no advance. If we want freedom we must have love as the foundation principle.

If only we could learn simply to love one another, it would be the solution of our problems, but we are apt to seek rather our own selfish pleasure or advantage. We treat life lightly, as though it were play, and forget that love is ever welling up from the foundations of the universe, for love is the fundamental principle of the universe. When we grasp this principle, we realize that we must hold true to the course and strive to advance, be it ever so little, towards our goal. Christ's disciple, John, said, " We love, because God loves us." (I John 4:19.) When we understand this love, we know how to love humanity.

When we meet someone to whom we are naturally attracted we say " I like so-and-so," and we think that we love him because of our own will-power, or because of our nature, but we must remember that the love which permeates the universe is making us love that person. It is God who makes us love in that way. Love is narrow at first, but it tends to widen and grow more and more inclusive until it becomes the love of all the universe. The more the world progresses, the wider our conceptions become. A man who has been concerned merely with his own family now begins to think in terms of his village. He becomes willing to serve as a member of the village or city council. Next he becomes interested in the problems of the prefecture, and is interested in becoming a member of the Prefectural Council; and then because he has become concerned for his country as a whole, he runs for election to the Lower House of the Diet.

Suppose someone has done us a wrong. We are filled

with a desire for revenge and all feeling that that man is
human fades out of our thought. We are simply concerned as to how we can take our revenge; we may even
plan to meet and kill our enemy. But when we look at
that man as God looks at him, that is, from the standpoint of the universe as a whole, it is undeniable that he,
though he may be my enemy, was born for some purpose
and is useful in some way. Thus, by trying to get God's
viewpoint, one may even come to love his enemy and to
be filled with an eager desire to love those who hate and
harass him.

Our love widens until it includes not only all humanity
but all created things. When one examines a little mouse,
he discovers that it is marvelously made, and when he
stops to think that it is designed by God, love for the little
creature wells up in his heart. That which is useless from
the standpoint of a part may be quite essential from the
standpoint of the whole.

This is the fundamental principle of love, and unless
one enters into the conscious realization of the whole —
that is, a conscious sharing of the viewpoint of God — it
is impossible to understand it. If you examine the fingers
of the hand each one by itself, they are not comely, but
when the five fingers are all there, they are both shapely
and useful. In the heart of the God of the universe, each
child of his is as necessary to him as the fingers are to the
hand. It is imperative to save each one, whether it be a
little child, or a woman of ill-fame. In the marvelous
design of the universe, not even a sparrow can fall to the
earth meaninglessly.

THE RESTORATIVE POWER OF THE BLOOD

Those who have thought deeply on this love are the
most useful to society and serve society as blood serves

the human body. The blood is constantly circulating in the human body; if there is any injury anywhere, the blood repairs the damage. We call this regenerative process anagenesis, but that means merely that we possess powers of repair and renewal as well as powers of growth. This is the duty of the blood. If there are no individuals who undertake the work of the blood, the universe does not move forward.

Love has this restorative power; it does the work of the blood. This work of the blood is called in Christian teaching, the Cross. This is the blood of the Cross. There is no growth without the blood, nor is there any possibility of repairing the body, but through the work of the blood even contagious diseases can be cured, and the body which has wasted away can put on weight. In the same way, those who have faults or defects may be restored through love.

Well then, if the blood has this function in the body, what is the work of those who represent the blood in society? It is their function to offer their lives as a sacrifice in order to serve others. Suppose that the oldest brother in the home is a profligate. If a younger sister takes care of her brother's children, and quietly and unobtrusively devotes herself to them, his faults are atoned for. Forgiveness becomes possible. A love that considers only its own advantage has no value to society.

Take for instance a labor union which makes an unsuccessful attempt to win some advantage from capitalism. When they are questioned by the police, the men disclaim all knowledge of the affair. But if the members of the union would hold together, no matter if they were defeated, and regardless of what sort of ill-treatment they received, or how cruelly they were punished, they would be fulfilling the work of the blood. Unless there is the conscious acceptance of the work of the blood, unless there is a conscious willingness to atone for the faults of others, there is no true union.

The blood circulates silently through the body. The people of this modern age are not willing to become the blood. There are many who want to serve society as the face serves the body. People today all want to become Prime Ministers. They all want to become " heads " of this or that. But if there is no one who has the desire to serve by healing the defects of others, in quiet, humble ways, even a home will fall apart. Sometimes when a man has been sent to prison, his wife will say she wants a divorce; she feels so disappointed in her hopes that she no longer wants to be his wife. She is usually convinced that he is at fault, and refuses to consider herself at all to blame. When the faults of others are disclosed openly, we disclaim all responsibility.

In South China it is the custom to run away from a dying person. It is said that this custom has arisen from the fact that it has often happened that a man would be given poison by another, who would wait near by until his victim was at the point of death. As soon as the man was dead, the murderer would search under the pillow of the dead man for his valuables. Therefore it has become the custom to flee from a dying person to avoid suspicion. But we must do exactly the opposite. We must strive to love the faults of men. We must try to atone for the defects of criminals, even to the point of shedding our blood for them. If a man's wife is given to shop-lifting, he must try to forgive her. St. Augustine said that even if a man's wife had committed adultery still he ought to forgive her.

We are utterly opposed to avarice. We are carrying on labor movements and village movements on behalf of the proletariat and the tenant farmers, but the capitalists are also human beings, and therefore, if they are making mistakes, we must forgive them and do all we can to atone for their mistakes. Society will not grow unless we take this attitude. On the other hand, radical groups often threaten to overthrow the capitalists, to " do them up." If these men shared the feeling of God towards these capitalists, they would be eager to save them, and they would be convinced that if they did not save them, it would be an inexcusable offense towards God.

If one man commits a sin, the God of heaven and earth is grieved and that is why we must strive to lead such a one to a change of heart. This was Christ's attitude. We are opposed to capitalism and to the crimes and sins of the capitalist regime, but we must try to redeem its defects. It does not do to take an attitude of pure opposition, or to feel that we do not want capitalists in our churches. We should not censure them for having committed sin, but just because they have fallen into sin, we must save them. This is the fundamental principle which should be the starting point for our activities.

What if the blood were to take part in a class war? If the blood were to say, " I don't want to go to that detestable old head. I'll go only to the feet," and thus start a class war, the body would die. The blood must go anywhere, everywhere, without distinction. So with love. Unless it penetrates to every part of society, the nation cannot endure.

We stand absolutely for the right of every man to live, to labor, and the right to character. I stand for the universal right to livelihood, but if we who are taking the part of the blood by striving for the reconstruction of society were to be asked to participate in a strike here in Japan, I would be opposed to such a movement.* The

* Dr. Kagawa thinks that strikes are necessary in the very early stages of the development of the labor movement, but that they should be

people must become conscious of the blood and its redemptive work. We have a share in this sacrificial service
to society. With the consciousness in our hearts that we
are doing the work of the blood, we must willingly forgive
crime, even the crimes of those who oppress us.

THE MEANING OF BLOOD

It was Christ's purpose to fulfil the function of the
blood by love. That is the meaning of the Cross. The
verse, " The blood of Christ cleanseth us from all sin,"
means just this. We must carry on the purifying work of
the blood by going into the streets where the rogues live,
and living with them; we must mingle with the prostitute
women; we must make friends of the criminals, restoring
and healing as the blood does, until crime disappears.
When our blood becomes impure, the blood of Christ will
cleanse it from impurity. There is in God a power which
is eternally purifying, repairing defects, and cleansing
once more that which has become corrupt. We must cher-
ish the example of the Christ of the Cross, who lived this
life of the blood.

---

minimized after it is thoroughly organized. When the cooperative movement is strong, the labor union should be a producers' cooperative in that
it has the service attitude toward other social groups rather than a con-
troversial one. Especially does Dr. Kagawa deprecate the numerous
strikes now being fomented both in Japan and the United States by communist agitators. In the beginning of his work with the labor movement
in Japan he did support some strikes, but by 1921 he felt the movement
had progressed far enough to do without striking. One of his associates,
however, a man somewhat under the influence of communism, started the
great general strike of Kobe and Osaka in that summer. Kagawa went
into it to act as adviser and help prevent violence. He was imprisoned.
along with a hundred other strike-leaders, at its close. It was at that
time that he finished the novel, *Listening to the Walls*. After his release
he informed the labor leaders that he would devote his time from then
on for a while to organizing the farmers, and advised them, the laborers,
not to strike any more. — H. T.

For this principle did not take its origin from men; its source is in God. Faith in the Cross, faith in the blood, means that one asks for forgiveness because one believes in the love of God. One has faith in love, in God's love. If there is a real intention to receive the forgiveness of sin through love, to enter the experience of being born again, and to begin a new life, one is forgiven because of Christ's blood, no matter what sins or crime he may have committed.

The reality of love is the blood. Love must live again. It must wait till it lives again. This is faith. Those who have been saved through the blood of the Cross must from now on live the life of the blood; they must live the life of the Cross.

PRAYER

O God our Father: We thank Thee that through the blood of the Cross Thou dost cleanse our sins, forgive our shortcomings, and purify us. Even when we are in revolt against Thee, Thou dost have compassion on us. Even when we blindly grovel in sin, Thou dost have pity upon us. We praise Thy love which melts our hearts, hardened into rock by evil heredity and crime, and purifies and revitalizes them once more.

We confess the sins of our modern age. The world today has gone deep into partnership with crime; we are repeating the wickedness of the days of Rome. O purify us that we may enter more fully into the consciousness of the blood of the Cross and forgive the sins of men for the sake of the new age that is to come. Inspire us to strive to build a road of righteousness that man may walk thereon. Create us anew into men and women worthy of having received the redemption of the blood of the Cross and lead us so that we also may be able to live lives of loving service, lives actuated by the principle of the blood.   We bless Thee for granting us redemption through the blood in this depraved age in which we live.   The joy of redemption is more precious to us than precious jewels.   Make us believe Thy mercy and cause us to stand on our feet, and bestir ourselves in cleansing our homes, and our nation. Give us the strength to purify our country, and our society. Cleanse our industries, purify us from the spirit of selfishly seeking the interests of our own class, and help us to enter into the feelings of the heart of God.   Grant that we may hold fast, we beseech Thee, in unswerving determination to our resolution to follow the way of the Cross.   We pray this through the blood.   Amen.